NO WAY! OKAY, FINE.

NO WAY! OKAY, FINE.

A MEMOIR OF POP CULTURE, FEMINISM AND FEELINGS

Brodie Lancaster

hachette
AUSTRALIA

Every endeavour has been made on the part of the publisher to contact
copyright holders and the publisher will be happy to include a full
acknowledgement in future editions.

While every effort has been made to recall past events accurately, the memories contained
within this book are the author's own and may differ from those of others.

 hachette
AUSTRALIA

Published in Australia and New Zealand in 2017
by Hachette Australia
(an imprint of Hachette Australia Pty Limited)
Level 17, 207 Kent Street, Sydney NSW 2000
www.hachette.com.au

10 9 8 7 6 5 4 3 2 1

Copyright © Brodie Lancaster 2017

National Library of Australia
Cataloguing-in-Publication data:
Lancaster, Brodie, author.

No way! Okay, fine: a memoir of pop culture, feminism and
feelings / Brodie Lancaster.

978 0 7336 3599 1 (paperback)

Lancaster, Brodie–Biography.
Women authors, Australian–Biography.
Women editors–Australia–Biography.
Popular culture–Australia.
Feminism–Australia.

Lyrics from 'Song for You' reproduced with permission from Wil Wagner, Pool House Records
Cover design by Jess Cruickshank
Typeset in 12.4/17.25 pt Adobe Garamond Pro by Bookhouse, Sydney
Printed and bound in Great Britain by Clays Ltd, Elcograf S.p.A.

The paper this book is printed on is certified against the
Forest Stewardship Council® Standards. McPherson's Printing
Group holds FSC® chain of custody certification SA-COC-005379.
FSC® promotes environmentally responsible, socially beneficial
and economically viable management of the world's forests.

CONTENTS

Prologue My Face in the Frame vii

Chapter 1 Unlearning 1
Chapter 2 Size Matters 11
Chapter 3 At Homes 38
Chapter 4 Tough is Not Easy 55
Chapter 5 Real Quality 76
Chapter 6 Dear Every Friend I've Ever Broken Up With 96
Chapter 7 A Hard Place 105
Chapter 8 Faithful 128
Chapter 9 He Lied About Death 148
Chapter 10 Where She's Allowed 162
Chapter 11 Body Like Velvet 181
Chapter 12 Held Back by the Love That Would Not
Give Them Up 197
Chapter 13 They Built a Statue of Us 210
Chapter 14 The Codes to Self-esteem 221
Afterword You Can Touch This Page 241

Acknowledgements 249

PROLOGUE

MY FACE IN THE FRAME

In the valley between my chin and my bottom lip runs a scar, fainter and softer than it was a decade ago, but still a place that make-up stumbles over, where beads of sweat collect in summer. I didn't have it for the first three years of my life, but I've had it ever since. In a daily diary, my dad religiously made notes about key events or conversations he had. He logged the day my sister hit me, I hit her back, and she chased me through our grandparents' house trying to get the last slap in. I tripped on the step that divided the living room from an enclosed sunroom.

I don't remember all the details exactly, and someone else might recall them differently, but the ones I can recall feel like truth to me. When he was a guest on the podcast *Another Round*, the writer Ta-Nehisi Coates was asked what his earliest memory was, and he reminisced about chipping his tooth when he was five. 'I have memories before then, but I know that happened, and I'm not sure about the other ones.' Like survivors of natural disasters on the news remarking how *that day* began as unremarkably as any other, Coates's recollection encompasses the way that everything is the same, totally forgettable or interchangeable, until something suddenly isn't. The permanence of an injury makes certain our history, because it's archived in our skin and muscles and bones.

The sunroom was once a porch, Mum told my sisters and me. She grew up in that house. I have a faded photograph of her as a teenager, wearing a tiny bikini, petting a black-and-white cat on the porch. It hasn't been a porch since I've been alive, but the step remains. With my sister behind me, I took chase down the hallway and through the lounge room. The step fell away from under me and I hurtled forwards, my tiny face colliding definitively with the old couch in the sunroom.

My face split open. My freshly sprouted baby teeth sliced through my tender face and blood poured out. I picked myself up and plopped down on the couch that had so recently betrayed me, curled up into a ball and cried into my knees. In a house filled with people, no one came to check on me for a while, because the sounds of my crying apparently sounded like laughter. When my mum came to look at my face, the extremity of the injury showed in her expression.

'I want to see,' I begged her, the words wet with my sobs.

'You don't want to look, darl,' Mum told me, stroking my thick black hair.

'I doooooo!' I was wailing as I stared at the reflection in the mirror of my grandparents' bathroom. They've renovated it in the years since, but I still picture the old scallop-edged mirror that once hung on the wall, and the image it offered, that day, of me perched against my mother's side, as she held me on her hip. The top half of my face was red with my furious tears, the bottom half was red with blood that was already starting to crust over. It was a bad day, but made better because I got to pick what video we watched that afternoon. I didn't have to argue or compromise with my two older sisters, or automatically agree with whatever they wanted to watch. I got to choose all on my own, and the satisfaction of everyone watching *Dot and the Kangaroo* at my request dulled the throbbing pain on my chin.

On my forehead is a mole that occasionally flashes with pain, not unlike Harry Potter's scar. It isn't present in photos of me as a baby, so I guess it just appeared one day in the exact centre of my forehead sometime later, and never went away, just like Harry Potter's scar. I wore my hair in a fringe and avoided sweeping it back from my face for years in attempts to hide the mark. Having moles on your body was bad, I knew, but having them on your face was worse. When you're a kid who feels weird about people even acknowledging your existence, an obscurity in the centre of your forehead felt like a flashing neon sign declaring THIS ONE IS UNUSUAL.

My family was on one of the few holidays we took together when I first remember someone else noticing it. We got ready to go to dinner in our hotel room, and my sisters and I took turns sitting at our mother's feet as she twisted and pinned our hair up in a series of buns, like the ones Hayley wore on *Home and Away*, or the ones that Miley Cyrus would wear, years later, as she dry-humped a foam finger at the VMAs. We were staying on the Gold Coast, far away from where we lived and the people I knew. It felt safe to let Mum pin my fringe back into one of the lumpy buns, exposing my forehead and the mole on it. I wore a blue tie-dyed dress with spaghetti straps, and my sister pressed matching blue glitter eyeshadow around the edges of my eyes. I felt like a cool and popular cartoon character – all shapes and colours. We had dinner at one of those nondescript 'Oriental' restaurants, where specific customs and cuisines of different Asian countries are fused together in a way that obtuse white tourists like us couldn't identify. We sat on cushions around a low table in a dimly lit room and ordered fried rice, prawn crackers, lemon chicken and raspberry soft drinks. As our waitress arrived with the drinks, she stopped when she saw me and yelled, 'Lucky spot! Lucky spot!' I didn't understand what she was talking about – was I sitting on the wrong cushion? Was she talking about my hair or my glittery eyes? She pointed to my forehead as she repeated, 'Lucky spot! One in a million! One in a million!' My parents love to re-tell this story, about how a waitress singled one of their girls out to tell them she was special, and over time the re-enactment of the event has turned the woman into a caricature, not unlike one of Steve Oedekerk's characters in the martial arts spoof *Kung Pow! Enter the Fist*.

Despite the thickly accented re-tellings, I love this anecdote. I hold it close to my heart and tuck it underneath my pillow to remind me that once in my life I was so special because of the way I look that it had to be announced for everyone to hear.

Stories like these were added to the long list of quotes and references that fused my family together. They acted like first-person pop culture, and held just as much weight as the movies and TV shows we quoted to show that we loved one another without saying the words.

We often preferred to look at screens over each other, and favoured references, jokes and impressions over honest conversation. I'm not sure my dad and I spoke much before I was a teenager, aside from re-enacting episodes of *Russell Coight's All Aussie Adventures* or having entire conversations using lines from Adam Sandler movies. I was most proud when I could make him laugh.

My sisters and I never unified around a common goal like we did when it was time to stake out the local Blockbuster Video. We agreed on a few staples that we'd rent anytime they were available; teen movies like *Crossroads* and *Camp Nowhere* were always near the top of the list. As we grew older, there were fewer and fewer things we agreed on, though. I was developing a keen interest in film, and wanted to study filmmaking when I left school, but the 'Arthouse' section at the Bundaberg Blockbuster, with its always-on-loan copies of *Mallrats*, *Trainspotting* and *A Clockwork Orange*, didn't offer much in the way of inspiration. One summer, without our driver's licences or much motivation to leave the house, Shannon and I pressed play on her DVD of the Hilary Duff movie *A Cinderella Story* every other day. Keen to break away from us younger two, my eldest sister, Karli, placed limits around the things she enjoyed so she wouldn't have to share them with us. She came home from the cinema after seeing *Looking for Alibrandi* and *Pleasantville*, both times declaring, 'You wouldn't like it!' It would be years before I'd see those movies and echo the love she had for them. After a family trip to the cinema to see *10 Things I Hate About You*, she couldn't deny our mutual love for the film. While she developed a crush on Heath Ledger and sought out the same shoes that his love interest, Kat Stratford, wore in the movie, I wanted to follow Kat's path of going to university far away and reading Simone de Beauvoir and playing the electric guitar.

My feelings for these people are innately woven with the things we consumed together at the time. Like the feeling of déjà vu you get for a particular line from a song playing in a specific place, connecting the threads between people and pop culture offers me a route to relate to them.

I was listening to the writer Roxane Gay talk about her well-chronicled love for Channing Tatum recently, and I had the urge to reacquaint myself with his breakout film, *She's the Man*. Typing the first word of the title into Netflix brought up another suggestion, a movie I'd never heard of before, called *She's Funny That Way*. It looked terrible, in that star-studded-rom-com-you've-never-heard-of-until-it-appears-on-Netflix kind of way. Of course I pressed play. The movie opens with title cards, accompanied by a song that made me slam my laptop shut.

It's Fred Astaire, singing about heaven and hearts beating and dancing. My mind fills with dual images, neither of which is more comforting than the other. The first is of Michael Clarke Duncan in the movie adaptation of Stephen King's *The Green Mile*. Duncan plays John Coffey, a prisoner on death row in 1935. His wish, before he goes to the electric chair, is to watch a movie for the first time. The guards – including one played by Tom Hanks, who bears a striking resemblance to my dad on a good day, but when he plays a police officer (the job my dad did for forty years) they're near identical in my eyes – show him *Top Hat*, the movie where Astaire sings 'Cheek to Cheek' to Ginger Rogers as he twirls her across the dance floor like a fuzzy spinning top. The second image is of my grandfather, sitting in the chair he always sat in, watching this scene with me, tapping his fingertips on the armrest of his chair and singing along in his sweet, reliable crooner voice.

These fragments of pop culture come together like one of those shabby chic mosaic frames that encases a mirror, and the person reflected back at me is the result of all of those pieces. My body is a cavity that has absorbed it all: the movies and songs, as well as the people and the conversations. On the outside are the scars and moles and hairs and stretch marks that serve a visual reminder of what I've seen and who they've shaped me to be. Whispers of my memories are imprinted on my skin and my face is bookended by things I've done and people I've met. It's less clear where everything ends up after it's arrived through my eyes and ears, but I know it's all in there, waiting for when I need to pull something out, or surprising me with a reminder of a song and a movie and a man, when all I wanted was to look at Channing Tatum.

CHAPTER 1

UNLEARNING

You will accept everything you hear as a child as fact. You believe the adults who tell you that playing with Street Sharks is for boys and suggest you stick to the dolls and Barbies you share with your two older sisters.

You will accept what you're told until you're nine, when two significant things will happen. First, you start at a new school. Then, when it comes time to choose what to play in the school band, you're dismissed from your first choice instrument when a teacher tells you that 'girls don't play the drums'.

You will know it's not true or right, but can't put your finger on why. You're a few years away from discovering Janet Weiss or Meg White or Karen Carpenter or Patty Schemel or Sheila E. or Palmolive or Tobi Vail or Ali Koehler or Maureen Tucker or Tennessee Thomas or Molly Neuman or Steph Hughes or Jen Sholakis or Lane Kim from *Gilmore Girls* or the bucket-drumming episode of *Broad City*. Instead, you're assigned the trumpet. You hate it so much that, after just two weekly lessons, you fake a stomach ache every Tuesday so you can instead spend the time in sick bay.

(You will hope your mum isn't too mad when she reads this book and learns, almost two decades later, that you were faking the 'sickness' that led to those expensive tests with a doctor who was trying to cure a mystery gastrointestinal illness, *House M.D.*-style. I'm sorry, Mum, I really wanted to be a drummer and my lips were not made for that mouthpiece.)

You will ask for a Gameboy and the Pokémon Yellow game cartridge for Christmas that year because a boy you like said it's the best one. You unwrap the game on Christmas morning and realise Pokémon is boring and confusing.

You will ask your uncle, on a trip to Italy, to bring you back a scarf for a soccer team that a different boy roots for. You've never watched a European soccer team play in your life.

You will pretend to enjoy so much noisy hardcore music because it's what the hottest and coolest boys on Myspace in the early 2000s model their lifestyle and aesthetics after, and you want them to think you're on their level.

You will tell yourself this behaviour is reserved for your teen years – and talk about it in retrospect with friends who similarly bought Nirvana t-shirts or masqueraded as hip hop fans to impress boys – despite the fact that you were a grown-ass woman when you requested an obscure and expensive imported '70s disco album at the record store because you knew a ~~boy~~ man was into the band, and then showed it to him as if you'd just stumbled across it. *What a coincidence! It's fate! No scratches in the vinyl! What are the chances? You should come over and listen to it sometime! I am relaxed about this interaction!*

You will spend your weekends watching your male friends play cricket or soccer, despite caring about sport about as much as you cared about pubic hair maintenance (then and now, TBH). You will have your mum drive you to every Saturday morning game in the hope that you can one day live out the plot of an early Taylor Swift video, where the boy realises his glasses-wearing, book-reading, platonic girlfriend is not like his skirt-wearing, cheerleading girlfriend, and finally sees what's been under his nose (or, in your case, in the grandstands) the entire time.

You will wish you looked like the kind of girl from this plotline in movies.

You will sit quietly after one particular soccer game as the boys huddle around one family's desktop computer and pretend to be girls on the internet to fool their friends on IM. You don't see anything wrong with the way they talk about shopping and make-up and nasty gossip as part of their feminine masquerade. It goes unquestioned and unremarked-upon that teenage girls like the ones they're impersonating are catty and vain and competitive. That cramped computer room stank of sweat and hormones and cruelty, but you were just proud to be invited, to be seen as one of the guys.

You will fall for the same ruse yourself later on, and say the most horrible things about another girl, not realising she is on the other end of the screen. You'll justify it because you were just stating facts about how slutty she is and there's nothing wrong with you saying that because it's the truth and if she didn't want people to talk about her like that she shouldn't wear the clothes or draw the kohl around her eyes or kiss the boys like she does.

You will wear it like a badge of honour when your dad calls you 'Muscles' as a nickname because it makes you feel strong and powerful, like a boy, not weak and mild, like a girl. Camouflage cargo shorts from army disposal stores and his hand-me-down t-shirts become your uniform.

You will begin waxing the hair between your eyebrows when you're eight. The dark hair that creeps across your upper lip will first be bleached a few years later. A boy at school will see it up-close and tease you loudly for having a moustache, until an even nastier boy chastises him for being jealous he can't grow one. Looking like a boy doesn't seem as appealing when they don't like you for it. You stop wearing the baggy shorts and t-shirts soon afterwards.

You will subscribe to a surf and skate magazine for teenage girls that prides itself on being unlike all the other ultra-femme magazines geared towards you; the ones that make girls feel bad about themselves by selling them beauty products and telling them how to be cute for boys and reminding them to be thin at all costs. *This* magazine isn't like that; it has a section called 'GIVE HER A BURGER!' that features photos of thin celebrity women who could do with some fattening up. *This* magazine is empowering! It is cool and edgy because it reminds you that acting like boys and dragging down other girls is cool!

You will call other girls sluts if they kiss boys at parties, but all you want is to kiss a boy at a party. They're sluts if they wear skirts you decide are too short, but you will dream of the self-confidence to wear those same skirts over your dimpled thighs that rub together. The girls, you figure, are also sluts if they kiss one another because they're just doing it for attention. You would love both a little of that attention, and to kiss a girl without anyone watching.

You will learn about feminism in an official capacity in high school, when your Modern History teacher shows your class P!nk's video for the song 'Stupid Girls' during a lesson on Emmeline Pankhurst and the white women's suffrage movement.

You will find something uplifting in the music video's depiction of the ways women are shortchanged – in the world in general and in the entertainment industry more specifically. (Even if, years later, you will understand enough to know that 'politically ambitious tomboys' and 'girls who get spray tans' aren't mutually exclusive, and thus find its brand of girl-hate-disguised-as-feminism repulsive.) You'll start to look at other music videos and TV shows through this newly clear feminist lens. That lens will be blindingly beige for years.

You will implement your feminism after high school in very black-and-white ways: by avoiding work made by men and seeking out work made by women; re-blogging flashing .gifs of the female symbol on the Tumblr blog named after your imaginary roller-derby name; inserting the word 'problematic' into every expression of criticism or dissatisfaction; reading *The Bell Jar* during a period of depression and relishing in the act of crying in public over a woman who *finally gets it*.

You will stop shaving your armpits the day of your 21st birthday, and the tufts of hair that eventually sprout will make you feel like you earned a bronze medal in the feminist Olympics. When you're invited to a black-tie event a few years later, you decide to shave the now-fluffy pits. It takes a few razors to tackle the hedge, and you won't quite feel like yourself afterwards.

The first time you pay a talkative Greek girl to rip hot wax from your bikini line, you'll remember the friend you made in high school who recommended you slather depilatory cream all over your arms because *boys don't like girls with hairy arms*. She had a boyfriend so you didn't question it; the logic held up. The cream was expensive and stank like a hospital and petrol station all at once. It burned as you covered your arms with it, something you regretted doing as soon as the chemical cream ran down the sink. You could feel every gust of wind or drop of rain in the pores on your now-bare arms, like every pixel of skin had a thousand nerve endings. You waited years – maybe too many? – to get a wax because, you reasoned silently, if the deliberate presence of body hair felt like a feminist act, what would happen to your politics when it was removed? You lay there on a plastic-covered table, your legs spread under fluorescent lights, imagining the tower of feminist credibility you'd so consciously built up over time come tumbling down with each follicle being yanked out of your swimsuit area.

You will watch films and listen to music by women that will change your life.

You will watch *The Virgin Suicides* in an effort to keep up with the coolest and smartest girls on Tumblr, and it will open you up to the work of Sofia Coppola, through whom you will then discover Spike Jonze. You'll feel immediately guilty because of how greater your connection to his work is, comparatively.

You will watch films by women that will change your life, but you'll also watch feminist films that you can't fucking stand. You would rather watch *The 40-Year-Old Virgin* on a loop for eternity than sit through some of the art films about vaginas that you sought out in the dusty shelves of the university library's AV section.

You will experience a crisis of identity and taste.

You will feel guilt because feminism *should* mean supporting the work of women, especially those with the talent and perseverance required to float to the top of the barrel of butter that is the film industry.

You will learn about the Bechdel test – a way of measuring a film's representation of women by noting whether or not it includes two women with names who talk to each other about something other than a man. You'll use it as a shorthand for good and bad, feminist and misogynist. You'll stomp your foot on a shoddy soapbox to declare it the barometer of equality. It'll take realising that late-stage Woody Allen films and *Twilight* pass the test (a mother asks her daughter about an antique chair in *Midnight in Paris*, and Bella tells her mother about the injuries she got thanks to her vampire boyfriend's vampire mates) – not to mention that the test says nothing of sexual, racial, gender or cultural diversity – for you to step down and reconsider using it as *the* gauge.

You will remind yourself that you don't have to hate work made by men purely because of the fact that it was made by men. It will take years for you to become secure enough in your convictions to like what you like because of the joy it brings you, rather than for the message your consumption of it sends.

You will remember to hold women to the same standards by which you hold men, while always factoring in the shifting rules women's lives operate under. You know that being born a woman means the goalposts are set farther back and stretched apart. And also it's raining on game day and the ball is deflated and nobody's uniforms fit quite right. And the referee is hungover and looking in the wrong direction. And also there are way more players on the other team who've been encouraged to play since birth.

You will remember not to compare men to women, because the game we are playing is rigged and it's impossible for everyone to play by the same rules.

You will feel fury rattle inside your chest like bronchitis as your close friend, a concert percussionist, tells you that he doesn't think his describing a female drummer as being 'good, for a girl' is an insult. You know the words you need, but they're evading your fingertips and you can't grasp onto them. You feel defeated and give him the silent treatment instead of trying to make him understand how favourably the odds are stacked for him.

You will remember not to compare men to women.

You will believe women when they tell you their stories about men.

You will not reward men for displaying basic human decency as though it were a revolutionary feminist act.

You will remember not to compare men to women.

You will need to be taught many things: not to equate womanhood with vaginas and uteruses; not to laugh at R. Kelly jokes; to carry your keys between your knuckles when you're walking home alone; not to describe curvy women as 'real', as if thin women are somehow made of vapour and wigs; to reverse-condition yourself and eliminate pejorative words from your vocabulary instead of making excuses for how they came to reside there in the first place. Understanding that your female-ness is not a strike in the bowling alley that is oppression – that other women are operating without the bumpers or the right shoes or a team behind them or the opportunity to get back up for a second chance after bowling a spare – will take a little time.

You will be indebted to the women who help you to understand and express intersectional feminism. You'll remind yourself that it is not their – or anyone else's – responsibility to hold your hand and pass on what they know.

You will learn that intersectional feminism is actually just feminism.

You will need to learn independently.

You will be overwhelmed a lot. Like, just so much. But that feeling will pass in time.

You will soon have a foundation upon which to keep building your feminist ideologies, even if sometimes the bricks form a secure and warm house, and other times they become a wobbly sculpture.

You will rely on your friends – mostly, but not only, women – as well as the music of The Julie Ruin and Rihanna and Nicki Minaj and Banoffee and Stevie Nicks, and the films of Nicole Holofcener and Christopher Guest and Gina Prince-Bythewood and Wes Craven and Joyce Wu and Cate Shortland and Celia Rowlson-Hall to show you that there is not just one way to be a woman.

You will learn a lot and unlearn even more. But unlearning doesn't mean forgetting.

You will remember it all, every step and every fuck-up and everyone else's words you quoted when you didn't have any of your own. The steps keep going, they don't end, but that's okay because you're not tired of climbing yet.

You will learn about privilege, and be made aware of the ones your white skin and somewhere-between-working-and-middle-class upbringing awarded you. You might get a little defensive about it, before the lightbulb goes off, telling you what a privilege it is to be made aware of privilege twenty years into your existence on earth, rather than growing up knowing you have a lack of it. You go to tweet something flippant like, 'what did the internet talk about before we knew about privilege?', and realise what a fucking arsehole you are for taking yours for granted, even when you're aware of it. You go home and write this chapter instead.

You will write your own rules eventually.

CHAPTER 2

SIZE MATTERS

My teeth grew too fast. They arrived when I was young and they got big, quickly. They grew with such urgency that they almost immediately took up too much room in their allocated space. Uncomfortable crowding occurred. A dentist told my parents they could be fixed to be neater, to appear smaller. They could be taken apart and melded back together orthodontically. But, she said, we'd only be making the decision to do that for aesthetic reasons, not medical ones. My big, uncomfortable, fine-as-they-are-but-even-better-if-they-were-different teeth are a metaphor for the rest of me.

I was first made aware of the world's eyes on me when I patiently waited outside the Scout hall for my first Brownies meeting. I was seven, but looked older. I was a head taller than all the other kids, and stood proudly in my gold and blue uniform with my belly aimed forwards to accentuate my fresh new navy sash, just begging to be filled with the patches I'd earn from all my special Brownie tasks. When the doors to the hall opened, we all filtered in and stood in rows. I felt a tap on my shoulder. When I turned around, the little girl behind me said, 'You're big.' It was a fact not lost on me; I was seven and almost as tall as my mother. 'I know,' I told her, smiling. She laughed.

'No, not *this way*' – she reached one arm up to the ceiling – 'I mean *this way*.' She held her arms out as if showing off a prize catch. The girls around her joined in the giggling that would permeate every Brownie meeting. I heard it when we did pottery and marched in parades and square-danced to 'Cotton-Eyed Joe' and perfected a recipe for lemonade scones. I loved my time as a Brownie, but it will always be the first place in which I was too big to fit in.

Every day I think about my body. I could be preparing food to nourish it; I could be covering it in Lycra and cotton and making it sweat; I could be removing it of any covering and exploring its every inch with my fingertips; I could be manoeuvring it through a train carriage with a backpack on; I could be meeting a date in a restaurant and wondering if the chairs will accommodate me comfortably; I could be dancing or laughing or standing still. It doesn't matter where I am or what I'm doing, the physical space I occupy is never far from my mind.

These thoughts have been there since before my dad told me I was too big to have a piggyback ride – a rule that didn't apply to my older sisters. They persisted when I was eleven and my middle-aged softball coach told our team that 'women like Brodie and I will never look like models and we're okay with that' (this was news to – and *not* okay with – me).

Before I'd even made it to high school, before my early-onset puberty finally blipped in sync with everyone else's and teenage nastiness hit its peak, I was already secure in the knowledge that the way I looked set me apart from everybody else – a curse during a time when all anyone wanted was to be the same. It was around then that I started taking in the cues – both subtle and blatant – that my body was not only bad and made me different from everybody else, but that it made me the punchline.

The summer that straddled primary and high schools, I went to the cinema with my friends to see *Shallow Hal*, the central tenet of which is that a superficial man could only fall in love with a fat woman named Rosemary if he's hypnotised, during a spooky elevator ride with Tony Robbins, to see her inner beauty. That inner self just happens to look like Gwyneth Paltrow. Rosemary's cannonballs drain pools, her underwear could pass for a parachute and, on her first date with Hal, a steel chair collapses under her while they discuss (what else) her weight and diet. These might be classic ingredients in the cinematic nachos the Farrelly Brothers have become famous for reheating and passing off as a filling meal, but they didn't invent the idea of laughing at fat people for doing fat people things; those plot points wouldn't have induced the laughs in that cinema – or caused me to shrink into my seat – if it weren't already firmly established that bodies that look and behave like mine and Rosemary's are so outrageous and gross and humiliating that laughing at them *should* be our default response. Marie Wilson, the co-founder of Take Our Daughters to Work Day, once said that young girls can't be what they can't see, and that afternoon in the cinema, I saw what I was reflected back at me from the cinema screen for the first time. And it broke my heart.

I watched this movie during the time in my life when I first started wearing a bra, when I was expected to pull on board shorts over my swimsuit so nobody saw my thighs touching, when my grandma raved about how much weight she was going to lose by sticking to a diet of lemon juice and paprika (never mind the constant headaches and short temper it brought on). Her daughter – my mum – would talk about how I'd never need to wear mascara because my eyelashes were naturally long and dark. She envied the thick, curly hair I got from my dad's end of the gene pool. I can't count the number of times she talked about the 'prettiest eyes' award I won at a baby beauty pageant. I always heard from her and Grandma, and from other family members and friends, that I had 'such a pretty face' – the inevitable 'buts' and 'if onlys' that followed always hung invisibly in the air after the intended compliment. *It's a shame about the rest of you* was always the only thing I heard.

My dad called me 'Muscles' as a nickname only a handful of times as a kid, and I clung to it each time – it made me feel strong and like my lack of physical femininity made me a cool tomboy, like Roberta from the movie *Now and Then*, who'd strap her boobs down to make her body as utilitarian as possible. I took after my dad physically – we had the same dark features, and I've been close to his height and shoe size since I was ten or eleven, when my growth spurt hit so hard and fast that my shins ached for a whole year. He would tell me I had big bones, something that always seemed both an excuse and a curse: it was why I looked the way I did, and why I could never look any different. Regardless, I clung to that rationalisation for years because it set me apart from other fat people: you know, the ones who *weren't* born with the thick heavy bones I felt for under my skin, the ones who *could* do something about being fat.

I had ingested so much fatophobia from the world around me that I not only compared myself to thin people and felt awful about myself as a result, but looked to people with bodies bigger than mine for relief. In the body-shaming Olympics, I was desperate not to come in last place. When the director Kevin Smith tweeted about being ejected from a flight for alleged safety concerns due to his weight, but he proudly announced that he could do up the seatbelt, it felt like a line in the sand, a division between Smith – who was fat, but could fit – and those who were fat and could not. Smith could do up his seatbelt, but were those who needed an extension belt (as I sometimes do, depending on the seat size and the belt-length and the layers of clothing I was wearing and any other excuses I could find because I knew asking for one was supposed to be a shameful exercise) deserving of the humiliation he'd endured?

Over the course of my life, I've dipped in and out of feeling a similarly misplaced – and, frankly, fucked up – sense of pride over being the 'good' kind of fat person; the kind that often eats vegetables and occasionally takes nature walks – you know, things that skinny people do. It was important to me that I was not like Rosemary or the other fat punchlines I saw on TV, and I turned that misdirected fear into my own version of fat-on-fatophobia. But fatness, like a belt or hotel robe, is not one size fits all. And I thought I was *the good kind*. It took me years of rewiring my brain to realise that any kind of hatred I showed towards other fat people only perpetuated and reinforced the judgement I was unsuccessfully trying to avoid myself.

That judgement manifested any time my volleyball coach reminded us that our jerseys were numbered from one to eleven according to size, and I was automatically assigned number eleven, the highest and largest. It was there every time I saw a pair of 'boyfriend jeans' – worn slung low on your narrow hips and rolled up at the wide bottom, presumably because a girl wearing them is so much tinier than the boy she borrowed them from – and blamed myself for being bigger than every boy I had a crush on. It was there in the audible sighs from passengers I dared sit next to on planes, and in the point of their elbows that were not accidentally jabbed into my side during take-off, landing and every moment in between.

My fatness was a flaw and a weakness, and every day was a reminder of that. It was the pressure point my sisters touched when they wanted to hurt me during a fight. It was the abuse teenage boys yelled at me as I walked to class when they didn't have anything to say but wanted their friends to think they were callous and wild (in other words, cool). It was the default reason for the rejections – romantic and platonic, audible or assumed – that I painfully recovered from.

I felt too big, too much, too weird, and I hated myself for it. I hated the way I looked, and the effect that hatred had on my mind made me reflect it out onto everybody else. The clichéd old maxim about being able to love yourself before you can love anyone else is a million per cent true; I only saw flaws when I looked at other people, just as I only saw them when I looked in the mirror. I had no way to express what it meant to be hurt by the dialogues women are expected to have in lunchrooms and comment sections. The more people around me hated themselves, the easier it was for me to do the same.

During the first year of high school, we were obligated to sample all the classes on offer, including physical education. Running laps around the oval in the endless Queensland sun was my idea of a personal hell, so I made a point to offer to take the class roll to the office at the beginning of every lesson. My teacher would ask me to jog there so that I'd return as warmed up as the rest of my classmates. 'At least do *something*,' he'd plead. I'd jog slowly until I was safely out of view, and then meander the rest of the way to the office and back, taking slow, purposely indirect routes. When I returned, I'd join in for the tail-end of the warm-up laps. While other, more sporty and less academically inclined kids my age were devising schemes to get extensions on their assignments, I became a master at avoiding PE. Our teacher would always forewarn us when we'd be practising long jump or high jump so we girls could make sure we wore our sporty microfibre running shorts to school. I'd conveniently 'forget' every time, and sit under the gum trees in the shade, reading a book, more grateful than ever for my pleated skirt – and every male teacher's ingrained fear of discussing skirts with teenage girls.

I dropped PE in grade nine, the first year we were allowed a decision over how we spent our time at school, and instead chose to focus on the subject pool vaguely called 'the humanities': art, film and television, modern history, ancient history and music. Studying history taught me to research and formulate arguments and my own, specific set of opinions; in music class, we studied the theory behind songs by Queen and Led Zeppelin and formed our own bands (I played the bass, and in our first/only performance, turned the volume on the amp down so low because I lowkey didn't really know what a bass was meant to do, but knew it was a cool instrument for a girl with black hair and thick-framed glasses to play).

I loved studying how the world worked and how artists reacted to it, but I really lived for studying film and TV. That classroom was the place where I could dream about writing movies and brainstorm who I'd thank in my Oscars acceptance speeches someday. In my last two years of school, I spent lunch breaks and late afternoons in our editing suites, my eyes glazing over as the iMac struggled to render the short films and music videos I patched together. We could choose what we made work about, and, as is so often the case with so many late-teen girl art projects, our bodies were at the forefront of our focus. In art class, a friend made morbid sculptures about how trapped she felt in her skin, while someone else painted a self-portrait and glued rusty barbed wire across the canvas. (I watched the movie *Ghost World* for the first time that year, and the early scenes in Enid's art class felt like watching a documentary.) Across the hall in my film and TV lab, we were instructed to make a short documentary about whatever we were interested in. My friend Zoey had recently introduced me to the Hilltop Hoods, an Australian hip hop group from Adelaide, and the other MCs and groups that made music in their orbit. I became obsessed with the genre, studying lyrics and consuming as many interviews and videos about the band as I could. I made a documentary that covered the history of Australian hip hop and featured a performance by Muph & Plutonic (one of the few high-profile groups who bothered to tour Bundaberg). I interviewed a teacher who dismissed the genre as just aping the racial and socio-economic legacy of American rap, and a local MC limited by what he could do with his music in our small town.

The subject of my documentary couldn't be less subjective, but that wasn't the case for my classmates. Bulimia, anorexia and self-harm were prime fruit to be plucked for these intimate short films, and their creators went all out; one girl had her (very thin) older sister mimic vomiting into a toilet, before throwing in a sheet of toilet paper saying BULIMIA. Making these films during school hours meant we were limited in our resources, so we relied on each other to provide interviews for our films. I tried to avoid featuring in the body-focused documentaries, terrified I'd be used as a worst-case example, the way news reports about obesity or diabetes use B-roll footage of headless fat bodies living their lives in public, unaware that their stomachs will be used to broadcast unsightly bodily crime or illness. My attempts to remain behind the camera were unsuccessful, however, and I was made to answer questions like, 'Do you think the high percentage of eating disorder victims is because of how obese Australians are becoming?' and 'What don't you like about your body?' Refusing to answer the latter question the way I knew they wanted me to (crying, yelling *everything!*, and running away), I dead-panned, 'My feet.'

It's not only fat women whose brains are filled with feelings of inadequacy and shame about their bodies, I know this; every woman has a target painted on her back by the Beauty Industrial Complex the moment she's born, and her life is spent dodging arrows. It was always that much more difficult, however, to articulate how you felt to thin people who talked about 'fat days' or wearing their 'fat jeans', who called themselves pigs for eating at all, when all you hoped for was to not have a stranger hurl those words at you purely for existing.

I was fourteen when I read Carolyn Mackler's novel *The Earth, My Butt, and Other Big Round Things*. I remember dog-earing it at page 281 – the moment when its heroine, high-schooler Virginia Shreves, finally tells her dad, in an effort to be more open and honest with him, that she doesn't appreciate him commenting on her body, even when he thinks he's paying her a compliment for 'slimming down'.

I love my mother and grandmother to death, but I've lost count of the number of times Mum announced, with an air of achievement, how she had remained a size ten until she fell pregnant with my eldest sister. My grandma proudly told anyone who'd listen that she was the thinnest one in the family. She did this during the first Christmas after my grandfather – her husband of 60 years – died, and she'd spent seven months reconfiguring a life without him. Thinness was always the trophy at the finish line, even if the race to get there was littered with heartbreak.

One summer, my mum and I went shopping for a new swimsuit and, to my surprise, she only suggested bikinis for me. I was – and would remain for a few more years – strictly a tankini-and-board-shorts girl, and was surprised at her suggestions. It was only after trying on a few awful triangle bikinis on my pale, fleshy frame that I realised the shopping trip was supposed to be like exposure therapy. My mum didn't have to say anything for me to hear the sentiment behind the experiment: *Show her how bad it really is, and she'll want to change it on her own.* When we got home – zero bikinis in our shopping bags – I walked to my bedroom, pulled out the book, and wordlessly thrust it into my mother's hands, open at page 281. She read it and handed it back to me. We never spoke about it and never went swimsuit shopping together again.

It would be years before I'd find the words to express myself in moments like these without the help of a novel. It would be more than a decade before I bought a bikini for myself, and longer still before I felt brave enough to wear it for an audience beyond just my bedroom mirror.

This swirling cycle of criticism and self-hate continued until I was well into my early adult life. I'd ignore questions that sales clerks hurled at me from outside dressing rooms when I was stuck inside, stuck in a dress, fighting back tears; I'd shoot sidelong looks at fellow fat women ordering food in public as if to beg, *Please order a juice; you're making us look bad*. I was like Tracy's mother in *Hairspray:* so terrified that someone would say something nasty about my teenage daughter's weight that I didn't want her to dance on TV. Only I was both of them.

During my second year of university, I was keeping a blog about local music and the mundanities of my fresh new life in Melbourne, when I got a comment on a post from someone whose username was FatAus. That was the day the cycle began to slow. I was curious and kind of horrified that someone would want to stamp that word on themselves, and clicked over to their blog to search for some kind of rationale for this blasé attitude to a word I'd spent my life dodging or crying over.

The blog belonged to Bronny, and she lived in Melbourne, like me. She was shorter than me, with a narrower waist and thinner legs, but we had the same big butts and boobs. She had pale skin and cellulite, like me. Her pictures showed her wearing clothes from the same plus-size fashion sites I frequented, paired with band t-shirts and second-hand finds like the ones I had in my wardrobe. We both lived in a sharehouse with cats, and spent our weekends seeing bands and smoking cigarettes. Bronny and I were alike in so many ways, but our biggest difference was the most important: she practised 'fat acceptance' and body positivity, while I still saw 'fat' as a pejorative, and couldn't have been more negative about my body and ones like it.

To this day, more than seven years after I first saw her picture through the computer screen, it's Bronny that I credit with flipping the switch in my mind that stopped me from seeing myself as unloveable, imperfect and a work-in-progress that would only be complete when it became smaller. It wasn't an immediate change, but a steady process of autodidactic research and healing, one that was influenced by someone who showed me that 'fat', 'beautiful' and 'worthy' weren't mutually exclusive ideas.

My friendship with Bronny grew online before we met for a drink in a bar one night, and it opened me up to academics, writers, bloggers and plus-size fashion designers that, over time, allowed me to treat my body with care and confidence, and see it as something powerful and beautiful. We'd talk about places to buy jeans and the politics that came with being visible and vocal about your body. She was the first friend I ever had who understood how it felt to stick to the safety zone of bags, shoes and accessories racks in department stores, and we'd spend time commiserating over the influx of attention any visible, vocal fat woman received from fetishistic men when they bared all (or, anything) online.

When I first wrote publicly about my newfound love of and confidence in my body, I was applauded by a creepy guy I'd met through a friend. In his congratulatory comment, he described himself as 'a chubby chaser for life'. It would not be the last time that men like him attempted to parlay my own body positivity into his sexual fetish for fat, but thanks to Bronny and people like Kim Selling, Gabi Gregg and Jessica Luxery – amazing women I encountered online through their writing on plus-size fashion or fat politics, who I'm now lucky to call my friends – I was able to construct strong and impenetrable defences against these men who were used to seeing women like us as vulnerable, desperate, easy targets. They took the assumption that people that look like me should be grateful for any sexual attention, no matter how unwelcome it is or how uncomfortable it made us feel, and blew it apart. I could spend (and, now, *have* spent) thousands of words expressing what these women did for me, but in short, they were the first people to tell me that my body wasn't something preventing me from being important.

In her short film *The Focus Group*, comedian Sara Benincasa (playing a food writer called Sara O'Reilly) describes herself with a list of things she sees as her faults: she's unemployed, overweight and single. She visits a bizarro group of independent judgemental hipsters who wouldn't be out of place in *Being John Malkovich*, and stands in front of them in just her underpants as they point out all the things she needs to improve upon. 'In six months, you'll be completely different; you'll be perfect, you'll be thin, you'll be happy, you'll be thin!' the focus group's leader tells her, mimicking the inescapable and unquestioned rhetoric that equates thinness with success and happiness, as he advises her on a meal plan that will make her successful. Successful, of course, is just another word for 'thin', because god knows you can't wear a power suit to a board meeting if your skirt shows any signs of VBO.*

---

* Visible belly outline, the unspoken reason so many plus-size clothes are shapeless sacks.

In some ways, the amount of work I do, the levels of success I (silently, internally) aspire to, the activeness of my social life and my insistence on documenting the way I look on social media and in public are small acts of rebellion against the idea that I should shrink, hide and minimise (and that I would want to do those things) – ideas I spent too long prescribing to. There is a societal assumption, which largely goes unchecked, that being fat condemns you to a life of sadness and loneliness, and I am actively and consciously fighting against those ideas every day.

Towards the end of season seven of *The Office*, during the final days of Michael Scott's time as the Regional Manager of Dunder Mifflin, Will Ferrell had a recurring guest role as Deangelo Vickers, a man who credits his professional success to the fact that he 'conquered obesity' years earlier. While saying his final goodbye to Kevin (who was the living punchline for years of fat jokes in the show), Michael forgoes a gift for the accountant in favour of a series of well-meaning but ultimately insulting affirmations: 'You WILL be thin. You WILL find love,' he tells Kevin. The two are connected, you see? Michael Scott may be a certified idiot, but the world agrees with him that fatness and loveable-ness are mutually exclusive properties. Kevin asserts, with surprising confidence, that he's perfectly happy the way he is, but Michael is quick to respond, telling him not to be.

When you're not thin, your life is in limbo until your body shrinks. As I'm writing this, I'm sitting on my couch with the TV playing in the background. In twenty minutes, I've overheard no fewer than five commercials about fat-blasting tablets, meal plans, meal replacements and other soul-destroyers masquerading as wellbeing. The women in these commercials grin maniacally as they shriek about how their lives began when they got skinny, as if their lives were computers and weight loss was the restart button. Like a grape that's been left in the sun, weight loss is supposed to turn us into the smallest and most pure, potent and condensed versions of ourselves. That's what we're supposed to aspire to, and that's why the idea of fat acceptance is so inherently radical: because the notion that being anything other than depressed and desperate to be thin is still an outrageous one.

At the end of *The Focus Group*, it's six months later and Sara's life has totally changed. Shot only in close-up, we see her on the phone to her dad telling him the good news: her new food blog has been nominated for a James Beard award and she just Skyped with Martha Stewart – she's a success now! The doorbell rings. The camera opens up to reveal a delivery person bringing her, not the latest instalment in a meal plan, but the greasy, deep-fried eggrolls that represented Sara's apparent failing at the start of the film; a snack that cemented the notion that fatty foods = fat people = unhappy and unsuccessful people. Sara turns around to climb into her bed, happily eating the egg roll. Her body looks the same as it did at the start, with dimples and a belly, and it's no longer equated with inherent failure.

Sara's progress is internal, something that is never a priority in the world of competitive weight loss that has come to pass as entertainment on TV. I used to happily and naively watch *The Biggest Loser* with my family, but after leaving home and discovering fat acceptance, the show left a sour taste in my mouth. Now, when I hear contestants saying things like, 'I want to be a better parent!' or 'I'm ready to be happy again!' or 'I need to look good at my wedding!' I understand where it's rooted: in the internalised fatophobia they've absorbed from living in a world that tells us all that happiness and beauty are not available to anyone above a size ten. I have never forgotten my sister's seemingly well-meaning suggestion for us to apply for *The Biggest Loser: Family Edition*, and her subsequent shock when I adamantly refused. At the mere mention of us applying, my head was filled with images of Classic Fat Sadness that would be demanded of me: looking sad while spooning caramel sauce over ice-cream; looking sad while sitting alone in a park as other people ran and laughed; looking sad while eating a family-size fish and chips alone; looking sad while inexplicably trying on a too-small pair of jeans. The most insulting, most damaging part of the show isn't its insistence on squeezing contestants into minimal Lycra for humiliating public weigh-ins, as if parading flesh in front of its viewers will inspire them to put down the remote control and run laps around the neighbourhood, but rather its universally accepted assumption that happiness and fatness are disparate ideas that can never intersect.

I wish I had encountered the fatshion community online long before Bronny found me, wish that I could go back and inject some acceptance into the years I spent being told the way I looked was wrong, without anyone providing either a contrary opinion or a voice of understanding. Even the bare minimum would've sufficed: a TV show or film that put a body like mine on the screen, and didn't send the message that someone would have to be hypnotised or tricked into loving me. That was ultimately why learning the basics of fat acceptance was so essential for me: it showed that my body wasn't a work-in-progress. I wasn't just a 'before' picture in need of a total overhaul. So much discussion about fat bodies is in the past tense, and comes from people who have lost weight. Their transition is supposed to be aspirational and motivating, while also sending the clear message that who they once were was not acceptable. Hearing from women who looked like me and weren't actively trying to change was so validating, but I wasn't going to get it outside of the protective circles of blogging and social media.

It's so rare to see women on screen at all, let alone in roles that have any substance to them, let alone women of colour, let alone women who aren't skinny and straight and super hot, let alone women who aren't all of those things and positioned as punchlines because of them. While fat people are by no means absent from the screen, we're often just there as a kind of shorthand for lazy/unfuckable/unworthy. If life imitates art, and the art was telling everyone in my life that, not only would I never find love/happiness/success/clothes that fit, but that I didn't even deserve those things because the mass of my body made me somehow less than human, how were they supposed to see me?

Anytime a guy dances near me at a party then turns around and laughs with his mates about it; or someone yells a zinger about rolls and bakeries out the car window as I walk down the street; or I see one of those stories about guys on Tinder sharing screenshots of fat girls' profiles to humiliate them, I have to transfer a portion of the blame from them as garbage people to the magazines that rank celebrities according to their body size; or the Rob Schneider movies where, 'What a huge bitch!' suffices for a hilarious catchphrase; or the characters like Miss Trunchbull, from *Matilda*, whose villainousness is entrenched in her heaving physical mass. Unless you're going out of your way to seek them out, empathetic and human characters with big bodies – bodies that aren't cues for self-hatred, like Martha

Dumptruck's in *Heathers*, or that serve no purpose other than being vehicles for Drake's thirsty rap lyrics – are almost invisible. *Almost.*

It wasn't until 2013 – the year I turned 23 – that the hypothetical idea of what I needed to see on my screen for over two decades became a glorious reality. Every 'you've got such a pretty face' – every back-handed compliment that disregarded or straight-up insulted my body – was all of a sudden on my TV, in an episode of the British teen drama *My Mad Fat Diary* in which the heroine, Rae Earl, fantasises that she can unzip her skin to reveal and release a thin version of herself that's hiding inside. Despite its extreme title, *MMFD*, which is based on a non-fiction book of the same name written by the IRL Rae Earl, is a nuanced and deliberate story that places a fat woman at its centre. And that was a goddamn revelation.

On screen, Scottish actress Sharon Rooney plays Rae, a sixteen-year-old Britpop fan living in Lincolnshire in the early '90s. We first meet Rae as she's being discharged from a psychiatric hospital and having super horny daydreams about her supervising doctor. Instantly, I knew this girl. I recognised this girl in my friends, in the women I followed on social media, and in my reflection in the mirror.

During the first of the show's three seasons, I was transported to so many moments from my own teenage years, playing out again like déjà vu. When Rae lies down on the grass near the boy she likes, tugs at her t-shirt, and positions her hands across her stomach in a subtle attempt to hide its size, I replay in my mind scenes of myself doing exactly the same things. When Rae struggles to find a swimsuit to wear to a pool party, I'm back in the tear-filled changing rooms, where I relive my terror at the thought of anyone from school seeing me without my clothes on. Rae all at once hopes nobody notices or mentions her body, and knows it's impossible to ignore. I couldn't relate to – or love – her more.

But the most revolutionary thing about Rae is that she is so much more than her insecurities and issues. She loves music and tells jokes. She's a supportive friend and occasionally acts out as a bratty teenager. She gets heckled on the street because of the way she looks, but rather than slinking off-screen (likely to cry into a bucket of ice-cream and leave room for a hotter, thinner star to step into the frame), the story follows her.

The show's title might make mention of her battles with mental health and body image, but ultimately Rae's weight is important to her back story – which is one of healing, learning to be loved, fitting in and carving space for yourself – but it's never more important than her obsessive love of Madchester bands or her kind, sensitive personality. She makes us laugh by telling jokes or rolling her eyes behind her mum's back, not by eating, struggling to walk, falling over, breaking chairs or doing other Fat Person Things. She is Rae first, fat later. She is a great example of what we *could* have been seeing on our screens all along.

During her interview in episode two of Lena Dunham's podcast *Women of the Hour*, comedian and *Saturday Night Live* castmember Aidy Bryant made my heart as swol as Drake during his Serena Williams phase when she introduced me to the term 'size-bitch'. To Aidy, who coined the term, being a size-bitch means saying – to audiences, both digital and physical, to producers or casting directors or wardrobe people or store clerks – that she isn't going to apologise for her size, and she'll be a bitch about it if she needs to be. Rae might have been the first character to bring a version of my specific experiences to the screen, but Aidy was the person who looked like me, did the things I loved most and vocalised the attitude I needed to have. She stood on stage during the *SNL* goodbyes wearing the same pieces of plus-size fashion I'd bought online, after performing in sketches in a body that looked like mine.

Comedy is always a dangerous zone for fat women. There's a thin line between the characters embodied by performers like Aidy or Melissa McCarthy, and the 'funny because she's fat' characters that Rebel Wilson made her specialty in the early years of her crossover career in America. After appearing briefly but memorably in *Bridesmaids*, Rebel went on to star in the a cappella comedy *Pitch Perfect* and its sequel, the dark comedy *Bachelorette*, and her own TV series, *Super Fun Night*, all in the space of a few years. In those roles, Wilson's weight informs her character's personality – to the point where her *Pitch Perfect* proxy is actually called Fat Amy.

Fat Amy hates exercise and, in the movie's uplifting climax, tells the thin girls on her singing team that she loves them because they have 'fat hearts'. Becky, Wilson's character in *Bachelorette* (which, I should add, is a film I j'adore with my entire, enormous j'body), is a mope whose friends tread all over her and tear her wedding dress in half when two of them get inside it and express their jealous disbelief that she's about to marry a handsome guy – just in case you forgot that a fat woman can't be loved by a traditionally handsome guy without there being some insidious subtext! (Similarly, in an episode of *My Mad Fat Diary*, a rumour spreads that Rae has 'a magic fanny', because why else would her cute, popular boyfriend,

Finn, be interested in her? I wish the image of an incredibly funny, understanding, uncomplicated and sexually magnificent fat woman existed more broadly in our culture, and not just as a confused rationale for how she magicked herself a traditionally good-looking partner.)

Kimmie Boubier, Wilson's character in *Super Fun Night*, is the butt of almost every joke (many of them about Spanx – I counted five in the first episode alone). Rather than taking the airtime to play with perceptions or do something truly new in this space, Rebel seemed content with telling the world to keep laughing at the miserable fat girl who inevitably loses the handsome love interest to her skinny rival. You know, because she's fat and that inherently disqualifies her from any romantic prospects!

More than offensive or annoying, these characters were so entirely disappointing to me because of how loaded they were with the potential to be *more*. I mean, even Evelyn Couch, Kathy Bates's character in the movie *Fried Green Tomatoes*, seemed on the surface like an unfulfilled housewife who found her assertiveness and self-worth at the same time as she began to get fit and lose a little weight, but actually the two were not the only deciding factors. Evelyn's friendship with Ninny, an enigmatic resident at the local nursing home, allowed her to broaden her emotional perspectives and engage with something beyond how pleased or unhappy her husband was with what she'd cooked him for dinner. Evelyn starting taking care of herself because of the dramatic emotional change the narrative gave her – her body didn't call the shots.

Aidy Bryant said on *Women of the Hour* that she is sometimes considered for roles in the same vein as Evelyn, in which the character assessment is little more than a 'low-status, nervous, hungry woman'. You can picture it, right? That character would be a secretary, or a nanny, and she probably wouldn't know how to button a cardigan properly. She'd be glum and useless and definitely have a litter of cats in her weird old house. I loved knowing that Aidy rejected roles like these when I watched *Darby Forever*, her first short film, which she wrote and starred in. She plays a woman who could probably be described as all of those things: she works a dull job in a fabric and craft store that's super beige; she's so low status she's not allowed to handle money or have keys to the store; and her co-worker (who is also called Evelyn – cool ~symmetry~) doesn't let Darby eat a meatball sub, even when there are no customers in the store.

The reason these character touchpoints don't infuriate and upset me, though, is because they're not *the only things* Darby is about. She's wistful and escapes into her daydreams a lot; she creates intricate craft displays that she proudly takes credit for when the cute water delivery guy notices them. We've seen enough fat girl characters who are *desperate* to scarf down a sandwich and can't contain their thirst for any guy who pays them a modicum of attention, but Darby is more than that; she's just practical and trying to fit her snack in when it feels appropriate, and expressing herself in the confines of a job where a polyester smock is the required uniform.

It's a radical act to put a body like Darby's – like Aidy's, like mine – on-screen and shine a spotlight on them. But what's even more groundbreaking is when you do it and don't make a big deal of it. Darby doesn't have to make an impassioned speech or overcome some injustice or humiliation because she's fully formed, fully realised. Characters like Darby are special and important because of how unlike the Rosemarys and Fat Amys they are. They can just *be*.

As Aidy proclaimed on *Women of the Hour*, size-bitches deserve to dress cool and feel glamorous just as much as anyone else does. Realising this, taking it in and really understanding it, has not only helped me to heal the years of pain I'd inflicted on myself because of my body, it also taught me to articulate how I felt about it. When I learned to listen to myself instead of the noise around me, I left self-hatred behind and learned how to practise self-care, and images of fat women livin' large have been directly responsible for this.

I was 26 when I saw Melissa McCarthy hoisted into the air to celebrate her fourth time hosting *Saturday Night Live* and thought, 'That is what I look like!' The same week, I saw Alabama Shakes frontwoman Brittany Howard command the Grammys stage and thought, 'She looks as strong as I feel.' Seeing Maddie Baillio take a bow after playing Tracy Turnblad on *Hairspray Live* brought me to tears, but this time they were proud ones, not sad.

Some days I come unstuck, though. When my clothes don't fit right or I run out of time to do something about my face and hair, my reflection becomes taunting. The criticisms and heckles echo in my ears and bounce off the walls of the bathroom. When I can't remind myself that they're wrong, they convince me they're true. I am a traitor to the cause and I've betrayed my fat-positive community when I wake up feeling shitty about myself and place the blame on my body instead of where it belongs, like exhaustion or hormones or a poorly cut skirt. It's a shameful place to be, knowing how the alternative feels but sliding backwards into self-hate all the same. I start to agree with the people who respond to the fact that I'm fat with, 'No! You're not fat, you're *beautiful*,' as though the two cannot coexist in one body.

Fat acceptance was not a one-step process. I did not get a certificate the day I stopped correlating body size with health or beauty or goodness; I am still learning and questioning and understanding. Like any course of study, some days there are tests and sometimes I fail them, but I know that the work and the dedication is valuable because of how foreign the other side of the coin feels now. Despite being fluent in the language of body positivity, sometimes the stray negativity floats in. It could be in the form of speculating why someone thinner got an opportunity for which we were both being considered, or wishing my calves were smaller so I could better pull off a cuffed straight leg. On those days when just *having* a body feels laborious, like a job I never applied for, I know deep down that I've made progress because the act of hating my body feels so unnatural. I can appreciate that it's not my default way of thinking, and the negativity catches in my heart and scratches the back of my throat because it doesn't truly belong there anymore.

The first time I saw a body like mine on the screen, I felt ashamed. But the first time I saw one on the stage, it was like my heart and my history with my body had been tugged loose and illuminated under a spotlight. *Nothing to Lose*, a dance performance by Sydney contemporary dance company Force Majeure, explored what it means to live in a bountiful, beautiful, despised fat body. Kate Champion, the founder and former artistic director of Force Majeure, produced the work in consultation with fat activist, filmmaker and artist Kelli Jean

Drinkwater, and with input from her dancers, all of whom are what an airline would describe as being 'of size'.

Where movies and TV shows want to show us what fatness keeps us from doing, *Nothing to Lose* thrillingly placed fatness on a pedestal (sometimes literally) showing the hypnotising, organic qualities of flesh and incredible fluidity and stamina of fat dancers. One scene required audience participation, and asked for us to rise from our seats, stand in front of a dancer perched on a plinth, and respond to requests to touch their fatness in different measures. Another phase of the show featured two performers who slowly ascended the stairs running along either side of the audience, trading the kinds of burning catcalls and insults fat people receive back and forth like degradation ping-pong. The audience felt split between 'people who have thought or said those things' and 'people who have been told those things'. I'm sure sometimes the two parties intersected.

A few days earlier, I'd seen Kelli Jean speak on a panel about fatness and art that was designed as a companion piece to the show. She was the sole fat person on the panel. Everyone's questions about language and body and discrimination were directed to her. As well as being horrified at how underrepresented we were at an event that seemed designed around the idea of our representation on stage, it also made me feel special in a kind of bizarre way. It felt like Kelli Jean and I – and anyone else who looked like us – were in on a secret; we possessed a level of knowledge and emotional expertise that other people were curious about and suddenly respectful of.

I had lived more than two decades in a world where people chose to go off medication that kept them healthy or functioning, because the alternative was gaining weight, a world where being ill was preferable to looking like me. And now here was a room full of people who had paid money for insights into fatness, and were being careful about the way it was spoken about, and the way we were spoken to. For once I felt special, and imagined how many more times I might expect to feel that way in the other years of my life. So far, it's been the first and only time.

Every day I think about my body. It doesn't matter where I am or what I'm doing, the physical space I occupy is never far from my mind. But I understand it more now than I ever have before, because I've both learned to love it, and un-learned the hatred I'm supposed to feel for it. When I get photographed, or when I feel someone's eyes leaving a trail across my naked flesh, my instinct is to flinch, to cock my head to hide a double chin and suck in my belly to give the impression that I'm slightly less fat. Overriding those instincts is almost impossible, but it's a task I've at least started to undertake. I've stopped referring to make-up as 'beauty products' because of what the alternative implies, and I've grappled with the concept of ugliness, and what it means to live as a person whose adjectives would accumulate to declare them ugly in a world where attractiveness leads to happiness and acceptability.

The story of my existence is the closest thing my family has to urban legend. After my sister Shannon was born, my parents, freshly in their thirties, decided that two kids were enough for them. When Shannon was a few months old, my dad planned to get a vasectomy and my mum went back on the Pill. Soon after, they found out Mum was pregnant with me (turns out the Pill doesn't get a chance to work if the person taking it is already suffering from morning sickness) and the following January, I arrived. 'You were an accident, but not a mistake,' my mum always reminded me when my sisters made me cry by telling me otherwise, or telling me I was adopted, as shitty little kids are wont to do.

I used to think I had to hide, that I had no right to want to look nice. Anecdotal evidence and a lifetime of watching movies with useless fat sidekicks and desperate fat virgins proved that caring about appearance wasn't even an option for fat people. After all, if it were, if we cared about how we looked, wouldn't we all be thin? When I let myself linger in front of a mirror in a public bathroom, or go all Narcissus while meticulously reapplying my lipstick on public transport, I am reminding myself that I'm allowed to care. I want to do it where people can see because I want people to know that the way I look is a deliberate act. My conception might have been an accident, but the way my body looks and the life I've lived in it since are not.

Learning to love my body has not been like flicking a switch; it took time to get here, and particularly nasty bouts of hormonal mood swings or too much time spent under the vindictive lights of a fitting room do their best to derail the progress I've made. But now that the syllabus is implanted in my mind, it's impossible to ignore the love I've forced myself to learn.

We are bodies. We are mass. We have more going on inside than you can guess from the outside. Fat is a loaded word, but I refuse to let it be used as a weapon against me anymore. It is a word that describes me, but I refuse to let it define who I am.

CHAPTER 3

AT HOMES

I am not like Tim Riggins, the football player in *Friday Night Lights* who was so proud to be from Texas that it became synonymous with his name. The place I am from is so far from being a part of my identity, that the person I was there and the person I am now don't feel like they ever intersected.

I was born in Bundaberg, a small town in Queensland. It's famous for the rum, sugar and soft drinks produced there, and is a twenty-minute drive from beautiful beaches. It has not one but *two* McDonald's restaurants; it is big enough that a drive from one side of town to another took some time, but small enough that the concept of 'traffic' didn't really exist; big enough that there was always someone new to meet at a party, but small enough that news of anyone breaking/hooking up was essential gossip that everybody knew within a matter of hours.

Despite spending fourteen years living there, Bundaberg never really felt like home. It was just the place where my family lived, and the environment I was in, before I could escape to a new one. As a kid, I was fat and friendly, with a good memory. My family lovingly compared me to an elephant – a comparison I *loved*, genuinely, and later inspired one of my first tattoos. A favourite cartoon of mine featured an elephant called Nellie who escaped the circus to find her home. Nellie's need to leave was just another reason to feel a kinship towards her. Years later, when I became filled with that same desire – to pack a trunk and GTFO – I remembered all the afternoons I spent after school lying on my belly in front of the TV, taking in stories about everywhere but here. My apathy and snark were reflected back at me by Daria Morgendorffer, whose family moved to Lawndale in the pilot episode of *Daria*, and who was preparing her own escape in the series finale, five years later.

When my sisters and I were little, we moved to Gympie, an even smaller town two hours away from Bundaberg, where my dad, a police officer, had been transferred. I remember my mum hating Gympie; she wanted to go home to Bundaberg, where she had grown up, gone to high school and chosen to settle as an adult.

A town built from the remnants of the gold rush, Gympie was nicknamed 'Helltown' and its streets stretched and extended into steep hills. My mum drove a Tarago van and my dad had a lumbering old Landcruiser Troop Carrier in a military brown colour. Both cars instilled in me a terrifying and lifelong fear of falling; gravity seemed threatening when you spent every day in the back seat of a long car driving up an almost-vertical hill. We lived in an old Queenslander-style house on the corner of a cul-de-sac at the top of a hill. When I wasn't performing dance routines with my sister Shannon to Paper Lace's 'The Night Chicago Died' and dreaming of entering our act on *Hey Hey It's Saturday!*'s Red Faces segment, or sitting in the gutter outside and using my dad's hammer to crack open fresh macadamia nuts from our tree, I was plotting an escape. I'd routinely pack my most prized possessions into the tiny wooden suitcase my mum had decoupaged with pictures of teddy bears wearing tartan bowties, pull on a hat and overalls like Shirley Temple in *Rebecca of Sunnybrook Farm*, and walk dramatically down the sloping street and around the block. Our neighbours, a Turkish couple my mum would chat to over the fence, would ask where I was going and play along with my haughty declarations of 'needing to get away'. Eventually, Mum and I were both granted our wishes. Dad was transferred out of Gympie after a few years, and we resettled in Bundaberg as I was turning nine.

From the moment we moved back, I proceeded to wait. I was biding my time for a decade at least, until I reached an age when I'd be old enough to drink and get a credit card and, most importantly of all, leave. Aside from Gympie, that place was all I knew, but it gave me a sense of homesickness all the same, as though being there was keeping me from where I should've been instead.

The cluster of buildings that comprised my primary school were designed with the Queensland heat in mind. Our classrooms and assembly hall featured high ceilings and massive walls made entirely out of tall panes of louvred glass. My classmates and I would take turns opening the high louvres using a long stick with a hook on the end, walking back and forth, cranking the windows open to let air into the rooms. Once, during a particularly rowdy school assembly, the principal told us to focus our attention on him. He said we might be tempted to look to our left through the glass windows at the garden and street beyond the school gate. But we mustn't look. We had to sit still and look towards him, at the front of the room. Even if there was nothing out there, he knew that just by telling us not to look, we'd be tempted to do exactly that. My eyes watered and I immediately started fidgeting. It took all my self-control to stay sitting cross-legged, facing forwards. I couldn't pay attention to what was immediately in front of me, though, when I knew that things might've been happening out of my peripheral vision, and I was too stuck in place to experience them.

The opportunities I had in Bundaberg felt finite. I could study accounting or nursing or teaching at the local university, and become an accountant or a nurse or a teacher. I could save the money I'd earn in those jobs – maybe spend it occasionally at the pub or on a new car – so I could buy a house to fill with a partner I met at the pub or at school, and have babies who would repeat the process. Then I'd turn 30 and keep doing the same things – minus the meeting and reproducing – until I died. I don't judge those lives or the decisions that led to them in the slightest – when I'm staring down the barrel of a three-month wait to be paid for a freelance writing assignment, wondering how I'll pay rent, and mindlessly swiping through Tinder, the concept of a mortgage and family and partner to share the load can seem idyllic and romantic; when I can't take a hot shower because the Melbourne winter has turned my plumbing to ice, I dream of the comparatively tropical winters in Bundaberg, where a jacket is not mandatory and houses are rarely-to-never built with heating even a consideration. Even the best things about the place weren't enough for me, though. I dreamed of being an artist one minute and a photographer the next. I wanted to see bands and go to film festivals and write a novel that would be turned into a movie. I wanted to walk down the street and go to a cinema or market or diner like Luke's in *Gilmore Girls*.

I know it's not my parents' fault that they raised three kids in a place where they could learn and grow safely, even if it didn't have art galleries or literary scenes to engage with. I know that stuff doesn't matter like good schools and weather and proximity to family does. They didn't put the walls up that kept me constrained, or design it so I'd hit the ceiling as soon as I learned to stand up. (They *did* plant the seed of encouragement in my mind that I could do and be more, though, so they don't escape the blame entirely for my desperation to escape.)

A year before my mum fell pregnant with me, Kylie Minogue came to town. She had been cast as Lola, the lead in the film adaptation of *The Delinquents*, a 1962 book by Criena Rohan. The *Romeo and Juliet* tale of Lola and her love, Brownie, begins with him following her through the quiet streets of Bundaberg in 1957. Unlike Brisbane and Melbourne, the capital cities that Lola and Brownie visit throughout the film, Bundaberg is un-glossed and wholly unromantic. When the couple first meet, it's during a failed attempt to get a seat at a tiny local theatre's screening of *The Wild One*. They dream of becoming bodgies and widgies – the niche Australian teen subcultures similar to American Greasers – and bond over their love of the Marlon Brando movie, as well as books by Jack London, and rock'n'roll singers like Bill Haley and Jerry Lee Lewis. Overwhelmed with how desperately he needs to escape, Brownie screams into the night, the clichéd but familiar teenage refrain,

'I! Hate! Bundaberg!' I had no idea that my urgency to craft a life and identity far away from that town was a legacy more than 60 years old.

When I joined my sisters at the same high school our mum went to years earlier, I started plotting a more legitimate kind of escape, this time without my teddy bear suitcase. The year before I started high school, my parents had separated and my dad had moved out. A year after that, my eldest sister, Karli, would be moving to Brisbane to go to university. They had exit strategies and I wanted one too. Five years felt like an eternity to wait. I'd spend my weekly, hour-long lessons in 'computer studies' (I might be a ~millennial~ by consequence of being born in the '90s but I nonetheless arrived in high school the year a solitary 'laptop class' was introduced as a guinea-pig-like trial to see if kids could *really* learn with computers) either scrolling through the archives of *Three Thousand*, a new Melbourne city guide, or researching private girls' schools in Brisbane, ones with plaid dresses and straw boater hats as uniforms, boarding houses for independent but communal living, and scholarship programs for high achievers transferring there from regional towns they hated. I wrote itineraries of all the things I wanted to see and do in Melbourne, and drafted scholarship applications and detailed pro/con lists to present to my mum in the hope of convincing her to let me go to boarding school.

My lack of affection for Bundaberg wasn't just because I wanted to live somewhere else, though; I straight up didn't fit in. There didn't seem to be room for me in a place surrounded by beaches and canefields, and filled with people who liked to surf at the beach or drink the world-famous rum that the cane produced. I wanted to travel beyond Brisbane or Bali, where groups of boys I grew up with took trips together to wear Bintang singlets that showed off their matching tattoos – tribal symbols on suburban white boys, or slogans like 'MEMORIES, SURF, MATES' branded across their biceps in Olde English font.

When ~~Muriel~~ Mariel Heslop finally escapes to Sydney and finds a job and a friend and a boyfriend and a Visa-seeking Olympic swimmer husband, she knows that it will all be lost if she goes back to where she came from. The heroine of *Muriel's Wedding* dreaded stepping back into the ill-fitting role she inhabited in Porpoise Spit, the beachside town that stifled her and crushed her family. Like Mariel, I can't help resenting my hometown so much because it was the setting for my worst years and most confused feelings. I was a human inconsistency in that geographic report, a blip that didn't quite make sense in the context, but had somehow survived in the environment regardless.

When everyone was at the beach or playing sport or doing other extracurriculars in a city that literally has the official best climate in the world, I was inside watching movies and dreaming of making my own; I was ordering English music magazines and albums by American bands that took all my pocket money and months to arrive, knowing that I'd never have the opportunity to see any of them live at the local youth centre. I was dialling up the internet on our family's shared desktop computer – a heaving dinosaur with half-a-dozen connected parts that caused the rickety desk it sat on to shake from the fan that struggled to cool it all down – just to spend nights and weekends talking to new friends on MSN or Myspace, wishing I could replicate the lives they lived in cities that had buses and trams and trains that could take you somewhere without needing to wait for someone to drive.

You can't overestimate the freedom a vehicle offers kids in small towns, or the restrictions a lack of one imposes. It's the reason movies like *American Graffiti* and *Dazed and Confused* use cars as tools to move the story from one place to another: because kids in those towns – and in towns like mine all over the world – rely on them to move their lives forward. Your social life depends on being transported, and if you don't have wheels, you stay still. Tia, Heather Matarazzo's character in *Saved!*, worked half-a-dozen after-school jobs to save up for a car, and, in a desperate bid for friendship, promised her classmates she'd 'come pick you up and stuff!' because she knew wheels were important to her flailing social status. My friends and my sister didn't start driving and buying cars until I was sixteen, and my spot in those back seats gave me a taste of what my life might be like after I left.

I never spent more time at dark beaches or parks or backyards or parking lots than I did during my last year in Bundaberg because our fun became more frequent and spontaneous when we had cars at our disposal. We'd drive out to the beach, or mindlessly lap rings around the main shopping strip in town. We ate our weight in French fries and 50-cent soft serves passed through drive-thru windows. One night, Shannon and I jumped out of her friend's car in the empty shopping centre carpark as 'Konstantine', our mutual favourite song by emo-punk band Something Corporate, played from the mixtape in the car. We danced together, giggling, loose and silly, in the car's headlights. We'd try to re-enact the performance later, an in-joke we shared, but it was never as easy and genuine as it was that night when the car took us away and brought us together.

It had taken time to ease into myself and my friendships during high school, but even when I was settled and happy, I knew these were far from being the movie cliché ~best years of my life~. By the time graduation rolled around, we all knew whether we would be staying or going. We'd sent in our university applications, our final grades were being tallied and all we could do was wait. I had been doing that for a decade already, so I knew for sure that I could handle another few months.

One of my classmates hosted an all-night party on her parents' farm after our Year 12 formal. We drank too much and lay in the trays of people's utes looking at the sky. We sat around fires and had half-slurred, pretend-mature conversations. We were masquerading as grown-ups before we had to do it for real. After five years of tolerating one another because we had no other option and respecting the unspoken barriers that kept us relegated to different corners of the playground, all the disparate social groups blended together seamlessly that night. We finally appreciated each other without cliquey division, but we wouldn't have the chance to again.

Bundaberg is where I learned to drive, had my first kiss and discovered the music that would become important to me. It's where my family gathers every Christmas, and it's where I know my parents will be whenever I need them. It's reliable and an indelible piece of my origin story. But I was never going to stay. Like Josie Alibrandi, the heroine in the preeminent Australian teen novel (and the film based on it, both written by Melina Marchetta) *Looking for Alibrandi*, who loved and resented her upbringing in equal measure, there was a ticking clock on my situation, before I could seek permanence elsewhere. Like Josie and all the bratty white boys whose punk songs about hitting the road and leaving towns and people behind were permanently playing in my bedroom, I wanted to have a choice in where I ended up.

When I got accepted into university in Melbourne a month after graduation, Bundaberg officially became past-tense. I got a one-way plane ticket that departed a month after I turned eighteen, and looked forward to restarting my life. I moved into a sharehouse and made friends at university, where I studied media and cinema. On the first day, I had a class in a cinema where I met Anton, with whom I'd forge one of the most important friendships I'd ever have. I went to see bands, and films that would never have made it to the multiplex in my hometown. It was hard and took time, but I crafted a life in Melbourne on my own terms.

I know we've unanimously decided, as a culture, that we are only allowed to enjoy the movie *Garden State* ironically. I get it – but there are nonetheless elements of it I can't not connect with, no matter how cringeworthy it feels to say that today. I'm sure I'm projecting on him a lot, but when Andrew Largeman hauls himself home to New Jersey from Los Angeles, I'm *sure* that some of the dread he feels can be attributed not to his mother's death or his life on brain-frying medication, but to being confronted with the memory of the person he was when he lived there. At home, with the grown-up versions of the kids he went to school with, he reverts to being 'Large'. He's back to spending free time in basements and backyards he thought he'd outgrown. He regresses, the way we all do when we go backwards. Going back can sting, if we open ourselves up to doing it at all. I've been back maybe a dozen times since I left Bundaberg for good, and each time makes me more certain of the possibility of time-travel: when I go back, I'm myself, only different, going to a place from the past that's the same. I find myself regressing back to that past version of me, back to who I was when it was my home. Suddenly, people of whom I haven't afforded a second thought become the topic of conversation. Who got married? Who's working at the new Kmart? Who realised they were gay after climbing out of the cesspool of pervasive high-school homophobia?

I'm back to asking permission to go out – not because I need it, but because I need to borrow someone's car to drive my story forward – and back to being a sulky brat when I don't get it. On one return trip, the frustration built up behind my eyes and I cried to my mum, hoping she would understand how backwards it felt to go from my hard-won independence to being back in a position where I have none. I was back to being the kid who wanted nothing more than to get out, only now the prospect of being somewhere else wasn't just a hypothetical idea; it was my reality. It was possible and tangible, but back home, it might as well have all been a dream.

The rites of returning are rife in films. People like Large or Tilly, the heroine in *The Dressmaker*, have unfinished business to sort out at home. It's as if that town to them – like Porpoise Spit is to Muriel, like Bundaberg is to me – is a box that contains the ghost of their formative self; returning means either opening the box and being possessed by the spirit of who you were so temporarily, or strapping it shut forever.

I am conscious of the cliché of these newly pompous prodigal sons and daughters when I feel my temper or exhaustion or frustration starting to build in my childhood home. When I was 24 and home for Christmas, I retreated into my room (which was never actually *my* room: now that Shannon and I live far away, it's became a guest-slash-storage room, meanwhile the room Karli now lives in was mine when she first moved away to university, then Shannon's when I left, before *she* moved to Canada and it became available again. The game of musical bedrooms is such that every inch of the house – and that one room in particular – is at once so intimately familiar, and so entirely strange and enigmatic) and wrote in my journal how desperately I *didn't* want to be another example of that trope of 'uptight woman coming back to her small town from the big city and judging the things she once accepted as commonplace based on her new set of standards'. Characters like Sarah Jessica Parker's Meredith in *The Family Stone*, Reese Witherspoon's Melanie in *Sweet Home Alabama*, Demi Moore's Samantha in *Now and Then* and Charlize Theron's Mavis in *Young Adult* all donned some combination of black oversized sunglasses, tight skirt and black turtleneck to show how far they've moved away from the lives of the frumpy, sweater-wearing simpletons in the small towns they begrudgingly visit annually (or even less frequently). They either surprise or avoid their parents; either cause or try to escape from trouble. The women I fear turning into are those caricatures of 'city girls' from movies who wear heels to walk in mud (there is always mud in small towns), confuse clerks at department stores when they casually drop the names of high-fashion designers, and ignore the pained looks on their families' faces as they answer their phones at the table to talk about spreadsheets.

'I'm terrified,' I wrote, 'that I'm going to become the family member everyone says is too snobby or busy to visit or keep in touch. They'll talk about how I didn't call and never visit. And I know it will happen and I will feel awful about it, but I also know with certainty that it's going to happen, because I'm never more unhappy than I am here.'

I was a teenager when *Garden State* came out, and remember it seeming so adult and unachievable at the time. It was filled to the edges with thoughtful people who liked The Shins, and had both easy access to weed and deep conversations in basements and heated pools. It occurs to me as I'm writing this that I'm the same age now as Large was when he went home for his mother's funeral. He always seemed so much older to me, with his turbulent family history and thoughtful monologues about growing up and realising the idea of home is gone.

My homes have been in four different cities in three different states and two countries. Gympie was the home that left no mark but ignites a spark of recognition when I pass through or hear it mentioned. New York was the home that hurt when I tried to squeeze myself into it. Like the family I found here, Melbourne is the home I chose for myself. The fourth home is my family, the ones who still live in Bundaberg, and the ones who have gone. The town is nothing to me without the people I've loved there: my parents and sisters and friends and grandparents, one of whom seemed to be there forever, until he wasn't.

My memories of my grandpa, Tom, touch every corner of that town. The benches scattered throughout a shopping mall remind me of how patiently he would sit and wait for my grandma to finish her shopping, even if she was gone for hours. If we got bored of accompanying her from aisle to aisle, one hand on the side of the shopping trolley so she could keep track of us, we knew we could go out and find him there on the bench.

He made his mark on the local bowling alley, where he designed and hand-built a maze of spinning, sliding obstacles for the indoor mini golf course. Going to the bowling alley for birthday parties and knowing the course was built in the garage around the corner that I got to hang out in made me feel like a local celebrity, and the garage an exclusive clubhouse. Then there was the RSL, where everyone loved and respected him almost as much as we did. He was famous there. Everyone knew him by name – or as 'Tug', his nickname earned in the Navy during World War II. Sitting down to a Chinese buffet dinner with him there made me feel special and important. He was a constant in my life, always painting the fence or mowing the lawn or playing tennis or reaching a lovingly cut piece of fruit into the rafters of his garage so the possum who lived up there could eat from his fingers.

He was always there, until he wasn't. I only made two visits to Bundaberg after he was moved into a nursing home. The first visit would be the last time I saw him, but it wasn't really him by that point. With one less person on the already-short list of reasons to return now gone, Bundaberg offers me even less than it did before, but it's still important because of who it gave me and who it made me become.

It stopped being my idea of home the morning I flew to Melbourne. The night before, I made peace with the beach – that hot, sweaty, crunchy place that was the source of so much body weirdness and the cause of the most ferocious sunburns. I drove down there with Shannon and Josh, who had been my friend since we were nine and I was placed in his class when my family moved back from Gympie. Josh and I kept in touch even after we went on to different high schools, and over the years we exchanged CDs and made each other laugh and were happily reunited at every birthday or Saturday night house party that brought together drunk teens from different high schools in someone's backyard. He was the first person I visited the afternoon after I got my driver's licence. That last night, we sat together on a rock at the pitch-black beach, with a towel wrapped around our shoulders. For the first time ever, being in that place, with those people, didn't make me feel like anywhere else in the world would be better than this one.

The first time I visited Melbourne I was sixteen, and as soon as I returned to Bundaberg I began plotting my applications for universities that would open me up to more options than I'd ever thought possible. I stopped spending my computer classes researching boarding schools, and focused all my attention on *Three Thousand*. It was edited by Penny Modra and I spent hours scrolling through photo galleries and reading the site from top to bottom like it was a sacred text.

After moving to Melbourne, I jumped at the first chance I had to go to one of the gigs *Three Thousand* advertised. I squeezed between the racks of a record store in the city to watch a performance by a band of guys who, within a few months, would be my friends. They'd share their beers with me and put me on the door list for sold-out shows I couldn't afford tickets to. I'd meet their friends and girlfriends to whom I'm still painfully close and platonically in love with. At that in-store gig, a woman came up to me and asked to take my photo for *Three Thousand*'s street style gallery. It was Penny. I told her I read her site – an understatement – and four years later when I was finally ready to release my zine, *Filmme Fatales,* into the world, she was the first person to write about it and let me know she thought it was something special. Seeing my name on the site felt like I'd come full circle. A year after that, when Penny offered me a job at the company she started after leaving *Three Thousand,* the circle closed back in on itself, and on me.

Soon after I moved to Melbourne, I was on the phone to my mum as I left class at university. She asked what I was doing, and I told her I was getting on the train to go home. 'No, you're not,' she said, 'that's not home.' We mimicked the same back-and-forth each time I'd go 'home' to visit her in Bundaberg, and I'd complain about all the fun I was missing at 'home' in Melbourne. Years later, after she joined Facebook and eagerly began commenting on every picture in her feed, Mum saw a photo of me with my friends at the pub. Her comment on it soothed the niggling feeling in the back of my head that I'd been a bad daughter for leaving, and in case I missed it (I didn't), she followed it up with a text: 'Don't know if my comment on Facebook got to u but said u belong down there even tho i want u here.'

She was eager for me to move back from New York when I was telling her how difficult my life there had become, and I was grateful to have her steady, dependable home as a sure-thing for when I returned with my tail tucked between my legs. Bundaberg provided an essential and familiar place of assurance before I was ready to collect myself and return to Melbourne, where she and I both knew I belonged.

Carving out a home here was not instant or simple. It took time to familiarise myself with the streets and references. I remember Bronny once saying that she wrote fiction set in the

Western Suburbs because she resented the way that mentions of Hollywood or the Lower East Side were supposed to feel universal, whereas Dynon Road and Franco Cozzo were relegated to Melbourne specificity. Reading *Monkey Grip*, Helen Garner's novel about the community in which she lived and loved during the 1970s, and looking out the window of the tram to see the exact same streets and swimming pools and tree-lined footpaths she framed the story around instilled in me a sensation of recognition and belonging. It didn't have to ignite that in everyone; it was enough that I knew what she was talking about. That familiarity felt precious.

When I spent that year living in New York City, I was in a place where everyone came from somewhere else. I could count on one hand the number of people I met who were born and raised in the city or state, the rest had succumbed to the city's gravitational pull. And so many of those people felt a connection to or nostalgia for the places they were from. I had none of that. I knew that when I left, it would be for good, and I would go on to find a home that was separate to my hometown. Aside from that year in New York, I've stayed in Melbourne, where my roots are now stubbornly planted. I can't imagine living in any other city than this one – not because I am stuck here or can't think of a better alternative, but because it has all I want and need.

I found my chosen family in Melbourne, and felt a sense of belonging I'd never had before. It put me at ease and made me feel secure to know that staying still and moving forward didn't have to be mutually exclusive.

CHAPTER 4

TOUGH IS NOT EASY

Not for the first time writing this book, I wish you were reading it on a screen and not a page. There is a .gif that totally embodies how I think my body looks and moves when I'm trying hard to impress somebody but don't want to seem as though I'm trying at all, and I want that image looping and jerking across your mind as you keep reading. Let me just paint a mental picture for you (ie give you the keywords to google instead of reading this next paragraph): it's a moment from Todd Solondz's film *Welcome to the Dollhouse*, and it shows Heather Matarazzo, who plays 11-year-old Dawn Wiener in the film, sitting atop her parents' car, watching her brother Mark's band play in the garage. Dawn is dancing and secretly hopes the band's new lead singer, Steve Rodgers, will notice. She's cross-legged and dressed in the kind of shorteralls with a rouched top that I dreamed about as an early '90s baby. She looks awkward and bizarre in a way that lets you know she tried really hard to make you think she looks cool. As the band practises nearby, Dawn is moving rhythmically from side to side, rolling her shoulders and wrists in a dance that's neither natural nor rehearsed, and the .gif plays online, over and over, looping infinitely into oblivion, until all you're left feeling is a sense of humiliation on her behalf. It's hypnotising, and way too familiar.

Every woman I've ever known would recognise this image of performing likeability. Gillian Flynn popularised the concept of The Cool Girl in her bestseller *Gone Girl*, which gave a name to the act of pushing aside your needs and opinions and emotions in aid of someone (read: a guy) seeing you as a romantic or sexual prospect. Dawn hasn't learned yet how essential this performance will be to her future careers and relationships; all she knows is that she thinks a boy is cute and she should adapt her behaviour so that he pays attention to her and other women aren't threatened of her.

I have always loved Nigella Lawson. She sneaks ice-cream into bed and keeps condiments on her bedside table, always hosts dinner parties with guests that look like they were cast from a brochure called 'Diverse and Sophisticated Friends Who Maybe Work as Art History Professors', and has the vocabulary I dream of having. Despite how irritating I find it to watch her chop vegetables with a paring knife, I was stoked when, as a gift for my 26th birthday, my sister bought me a ticket to see Nigella in conversation when she visited Melbourne. I took my seat a full hour before Nigella was due to appear and began counting down the minutes until I would set eyes on her. Before she arrived on stage, though, she had to be introduced by the evening's host. Rather than detail the touch-points in Nigella's career – like, say, her past as a journalist, or the time she spent working as a chambermaid in Italy (a bizarrely specific experience she drops casually into episodes of her TV cooking shows anytime she's preparing pasta or wantonly tearing balls of mozzarella into chunks, but gives absolutely zero context for) – the host, who is a food writer and TV cook herself, announced her in an insulting and simplistic way that only reinforced painful and poisonous attitudes women are encouraged to display towards one another: 'She's clever, she's beautiful, she's intelligent, and she's good in the kitchen. We should hate her!' A few laughs filtered through the room as I bristled in my seat, trying to hold in a groan, not just because of the implication of those words, but that they would likely go unchecked and unquestioned. After all, if a woman is traditionally hot, we *should* be wary; if she's hot and sweet, we *should* be suspicious; if she's hot, sweet and skilled in what she does, she's the fucking enemy. These are apparently just facts we all accept, and Nigella is just somebody all women should despise because of some neanderthal idea of female competitiveness.

If Nigella were a character in a rom-com, chances are she wouldn't have any female friends. Women would be threatened by her beauty and jealous of her sex appeal and for that, she would need to be punished. She'd slip on a stray slice of mango in front of a handsome man, or she'd set the kitchen on fire during a dinner party, or her dog would shit in an important guest's shoe. Because of her beauty and her success, *something* embarrassing would have to happen to make her likeable to other characters, and for the hypothetical movie's audience to be on her side. Movies are drunk with this concept.

Anna's white t-shirt is stained with orange juice when we meet her in *Notting Hill*, effectively minimising her movie star power; Mary stumbles and catches her high heel in a sewer grate in *The Wedding Planner*, rendering this otherwise highly capable woman totally meek and vulnerable; Bridget Jones is a drunk mess doing embarrassing karaoke at her office Christmas party when Daniel first notices her. Yes, two of those three examples could be considered 'meet-cutes with Hugh Grant', but they feed into something more pervasive and disabling: the humiliation women experience at the hands of a culture that is threatened by their capability and beauty. If a successful and beautiful and charming woman on screen is going to have any kind of romantic success, she needs to be neutralised first. She must fall over or hit her head or get bovine-strength anaesthetics at the dentist and drool all over her briefcase. She must be perfect, but not threatening, otherwise we can't cheer when the male lead falls for her.

And, yeah, what about those male leads? Surely the same rules apply to them as well? Hahahahahaha shut up. You know they don't! They are ultra-capable supermen with terrible hair-cuts, high-flying jobs at in-demand architecture firms, and no emotional intelligence! They're basically perfect! In fact, there's an old screenwriting rule (that has informed the structure of an incredible number of films) offering handy hints on ensuring your male lead is liked by audiences no matter what he does or says. The rule is called 'Save the Cat', and was popularised by the late screenwriter Blake Snyder in his book of the same name.

The basic premise is thus: to make a male character likeable, a screenwriter should have him 'save the cat' – you know, do a good deed like rescuing a pet stuck in a tree or helping an old lady carry her shopping or, I don't know, not abusing a woman when he gets in a bad mood – to get you on his side. He should do this in the first act of the film because if he's shown you that one human character trait, he's got you hooked. After that, you'll root for him no matter what he does next. It's the official name for the, 'Aw, come on kid,' moment a hero like Indiana Jones or Aladdin or Don Draper has after doing something disgusting or morally corrupt or insulting.

This is both a screenwriting trope (one that, now you're aware of it, you'll begin seeing *everywhere*) and a reminder that gender imbalance exists beyond the measly number of women working behind the scenes; we'll watch dudes do just about anything if we know we're supposed to be rooting for them, but we rarely offer our female protagonists the same allowance. A man needs to do one good deed in the opening scenes of a film to get you on-side; women need to either totally change who they are at their core, or suffer an instance of humiliation or emotional vulnerability to have any hope of doing the same.

In 2011, Tad Friend wrote a *New Yorker* profile on the actor Anna Faris, who's perfected a comedy style that offsets her classic beauty with bizarre and unsettling affectations and often disturbed characters. Because of this apparently jarring combination between 'hot bod' and 'weird brain', profiles of Faris tend to sound like she's doing something revolutionary, instead of just playing characters that do more than textbook -hot girl things- like, I don't know, talking shit about her friends or inventing elaborate excuses to get out of homework. You know, the stuff dumb hot bitches are always doing! I guess having someone who looks like Faris doing anything more exciting or genuine, by Hollywood standards, is actually pretty revolutionary. In the piece, titled 'Funny Like a Guy', Friend quoted an unnamed female screenwriter who unpacked the reality for women on screen and those of us who watch them in a painfully demoralising summary: 'To make a woman adorable you have to defeat her at the beginning,' she said. 'With male characters, smoking pot, getting drunk, and lying around watching porn is likeable; with females, the same conduct is hateful. So funny women must not only be gorgeous; they must fall down and then sob, knowing it's all their fault.' Granted, in the years since this profile was first published we've been blessed with not only more female characters on our screens, but more complicated representations of what women are and can be. Between the always blazed Abbi and Ilana on *Broad City*, the mischievous titular character on *Loosely Exactly Nicole* and the lost sisters on *Togetherness*, there are more options than ever to watch women having adventures and sex and emotional breakdowns. But one thing is still essential: we need to like them.

In 2015 I stood on stage at the Sydney Opera House to give a TEDxTalk, the first words of which were: 'Before I get started, I need you to know how much I want you to like me.' It got a laugh, which I didn't expect, because I was being totally serious. I was going to stand on that stage wearing a wireless Britney microphone for ten whole minutes talking about this very phenomenon – one that I had started to see was a trap masquerading as a goal – mentioning some of the examples and ideas you've just read, making an attempt at dismantling the idea of likeability, and questioning how we can view female characters (and the women in our real lives) differently when we remove the expectation for them to please and appease. I needed to open my talk with that line, because it was essential that the audience was on my side, because if they thought I was just a whingeing, mouthy bitch I would've been toast. Nobody was going to listen to what I had to say about likeability if they didn't like me first.

Paris Geller knew this. When Rory Gilmore's academic rival-turned-reluctant-friend in *Gilmore Girls* ran for class president and her friends conducted an informal poll of their classmates to gauge how she was tracking, Paris learned that the student body overwhelmingly believed she was the most qualified and competent nominee for the position. She was a shoe-in, right? Not quite. The poll also considered likeability, and that was where Paris's campaign came unstuck. Almost 100 per cent of her classmates said their fear of Paris would impact their voting decision. She is smart and determined. She valued nothing more than academic and professional success, but people didn't like that. 'They think I'm the best for the job, but they don't want to go to the mall with me so they won't vote for me and that means I'm going to lose,' she cried to Rory, begging the mild bookworm to join her campaign and help to secure the pleasant vote.

It's not cool for women to verbalise the unspoken rules they resent being made to follow. The internet has made it easier to find people with whom you can commiserate or feel a sense of community, but it's also opened us up to endless opportunities to be called fat sluts – something that happened in the days after my TEDxTalk was posted on YouTube.

After delivering the talk and following it up with a number of margaritas, I flew home to Melbourne and, within a few weeks, had finally settled back into my daily rhythm and routine. The adrenaline had subsided, and I no longer spent every shower I took reciting the trickier parts of my talk to an audience of mouldy tiles and expired Lush face masks. I woke up one morning to see a video of my talk was being shared online, and was so ecstatic I took myself out to celebrate. I got my make-up done at a department store and splashed out and bought a concealer, then visited a homewares store to buy a semi-fancy quilt I did not need. By the time I got home from my shopping trip, I looked at the video again and scrolled down, and this time I was less than thrilled. I know the mantra of 'don't read the comments' is an essential reminder for so many women who dare to voice their experiences online, but that didn't help me much when I saw I was being called a disgusting bitch who needed to get on the treadmill if I ever wanted to be liked by a man. Despite delivering a talk I truly believed in, all about how it doesn't matter if a woman is liked if her work can stand for itself and how a system that says otherwise sets us up to fail, I felt broken to see that people hated me for saying it. Despite the nice comments and messages I received, I crawled under my new quilt and willed that day to end.

Women like Nigella Lawson have to work hard to assert that they possess basic intelligence and personalities that are often ignored in favour of talking about their bodies, meanwhile women who aren't awarded the sex symbol medal have to work twice as hard to be listened to by people who aren't attracted to us. Whether or not someone agrees with what we're saying doesn't matter if they don't like the way we look, and this divide – between 'sexy and underestimated' and 'unattractive and ignored' – is one that it's near-impossible to navigate. No matter what we have to say, it'll never be as important as how we look.

This idea was clarified in an episode of the FX drama series *American Crime Story: The People v. O.J. Simpson.* (Which, at the time of writing, I am fucking obsessed with – I can't wait to see how it ends!) The episode, titled 'Marcia, Marcia, Marcia', examines the myriad ways that public defender Marcia Clark's appearance became as much a part of the murder trial as the size of Simpson's leather glove. Everything from the length of her skirt and the degree of her curls, to her worth as a mother and woman is called into question in the tabloids and on TV and radio during the televised trial. And – spoiler alert – she never comes out on top. When she tries to play the game by adopting new hairstyles or, at her boss's suggestion, performing in a more friendly manner in *the courtroom of a murder trial,* she learns that the game is rigged. Nothing she does will make her the hero, and she's both resentful that she's made to want that title in the first place, and upset that she can't earn it no matter how hard she tries. In light of fresh new attention being poured on the case and a mildly less horrifyingly sexist audience watching a dramatised version of it in 2016, Marcia became a regular feature on talk shows and in magazines. Hosts like Ellen DeGeneres seemed stoked to point out that Marcia was being offered the chance to rewrite the judgement and criticism that plagued her during the ten-month trial, with the subtext being: *we treat women so much better now than we did then*!

We don't really though, and Dana Brody knows it. The character on the TV show *Homeland* was sixteen when her father was found captured in Iraq after eight years as a prisoner of war in the first episode of the show. She would've been about seventeen by the time the world learned that (spoiler alert!) he had, in fact, been turned by al Qaeda – something Dana held shaky suspicions about thanks to her keen and emotional observations of her dad's behaviour. I loved that first season of *Homeland*, and, despite its dramatic stumbles, stayed glued to the subsequent two seasons before abandoning the show. I gave up partly because Dana, who had almost provided our eyes on the show, as the one character who seemed to notice and be impacted by the fucked-up behaviour of all the adults around her, was written off abruptly. But the more I talked about *Homeland*, the more I realised no one shared my view on the teenager: every conversation I had about the show (and there were a lot; I was obsessed) inevitably came around to how annoying and whiny and distracting she was. Dana's family was crumbling around her, she was institutionalised, she rebelled, and she felt very convincingly real, teenage feelings. Yet the common discourse couldn't escape how irritating it was when she yelled and sulked and demanded to know what was going on in her family. Her character was written off before she could do more than just react, or become a character with any real ambition or agency. The world likely would've still hated her even if she had.

I don't know Anne Hathaway, but looking at the roles she takes and the ways in which she's personally criticised in the press, when I look at her I feel like I'm watching someone who is coming last in a race she has no interest in running.

Somewhere around 2012, Hathaway was universally accepted as the grating try-hard theatre kid and began to be framed in opposition to Jennifer Lawrence, whose girl-next-door, cool-without-trying persona saw her win hearts and, the next year, an Oscar. Where Jennifer tripped in her capacious gown on her way to collect her award, cementing her relatable goofball image, the cut of Anne's sleek Prada dress made her the source of countless jokes, and even propelled her to issue a public apology to Valentino, the designer whose dress she had originally intended to wear to the ceremony.

She seemed too rehearsed on stage, she seemed to *want it* too much, she seemed desperate to make us like her, that dress made it look like her nipples were sharp – criticising Anne Hathaway became a public sport and there were no penalties for overstepping personal barriers in an effort to score points against her.

Anne has been a central figure in my image of how women perform – or reject – likeability on screen since she starred in *The Devil Wears Prada* as Andy, the reluctant (and, frankly, pretty bratty) assistant to Meryl Streep's iconic Miranda Priestly, a boss so bristly and direct that she inspired fear in anyone who encountered her. Despite hating her job, Andy respects Miranda. When her boyfriend talks shit about Miranda, Andy defends her by pointing out the glaringly obvious fact that, 'if Miranda were a man, no one would notice anything except how great she is at her job'.

Less than a decade after playing a character on the receiving end of a villainous female boss's demands, Anne did a one-eighty and took on a role in the same vein as Miranda Priestly. In Nancy Meyers's 2015 film *The Intern*, she plays Jules, the founder of an online fashion start-up. She decides to hire senior interns – including Ben, played by Robert De Niro – around the same time as her company is expanding beyond her capabilities and her stay-at-home husband is feeling so emasculated by her success that he's driven to cheat on her.

When we meet Jules, she's on the phone with a customer, giving her personal assurance that the customer's enquiry will be resolved, and offering her personal cell-phone number to the baffled and upset bride. She seems like a dedicated and committed customer service rep – a character not too far above the station of the one she played in *The Devil Wears Prada*. When her harried assistant runs over to remind her of a string of urgent meetings, emails and phone calls, though, we realise: *oh, she the boss now!*

The movie is set in the start-up world and sweetly tries to articulate what happens in that world for an audience of Nancy Meyers viewers, like Nora Ephron did when she patiently explained the concept of blogging for *Julie & Julia*'s audience. We know that Jules is good at her job because she says faux-insightful things about website traffic and hero images to a staff of graphic designers. She rides from one side of their office (a converted warehouse in Brooklyn, obvi) on a bike, because she's the cool young hip fashion internet boss!

Of course, being the boss – especially a young, female one in the tech world – comes with its own unique set of problems, ones that Jules is able to articulate in a series of lengthy monologues to Ben as their relationship strengthens. While the two are away on a work trip together, she opens up about the fact that her husband is cheating on her with another mother from their daughter's pre-school – a mother who, we have to assume, does not run a successful company and distractedly mutter through conversations with her parents, like Jules does. It's during this emotional autopsy that Jules sums up everything she, and all working women (including the severely misunderstood Miranda Priestly) think and fear about how their work will impact on their relationships: 'It's classic though, isn't it? The successful wife, the husband who feels like his manhood is threatened so he acts out . . . part of me was even expecting this.'

Jules's emotional and astute reading of her scenario tells us that she is acutely familiar with the Curse of the Successful Woman, and even when her relationship was buoyant (as opposed to crashing onto the rocks) she knew there was a time limit on it. The footnote to life as a woman who prioritises her work is frustratingly predictable, and even when she's admitting her greatest fears, ones rooted in reality – about him getting remarried and her, the difficult one, potentially being single forever – ones that are relatable to every successful working woman – she's still apologising for verbalising the fears that keep her awake at night instead of letting them silently suffocate her.

Watching that scene felt like the ghost of Miranda Priestly had flown in the window and was clicking her tongue at Jules from across the room. In a parallel universe, they'd had this conversation before, when Andy found Miranda in her Paris hotel room, tear-streaked face forming the backdrop for a request to reorganise the seating chart for an event because her husband wouldn't be joining her there, after all. 'Another divorce splashed across page six,' Miranda murmurs. 'I can just imagine what they're gonna write about me: The Dragon Lady, *career-obsessed*.' That's it; she articulates a woman's greatest sin before the thought trails off and it's back to thoughts of her daughters and where Donatella Versace will sit at the event. Miranda was never one for an emotional monologue.

Jules and Ben are on this work trip to meet and vet potential CEOs. She's been advised to hire someone (a man) to take over the corporate interests of the company she founded, partly in an effort to save her marriage. Ben is, bizarrely, the feminist voice of reason throughout the film; Nancy Meyers really un-subtly stuffed De Niro's infamously slack mouth with all the uplifting, pro-women speeches about how Jules *should* be allowed to enjoy her success without worrying that her husband will cheat as a result. When he goes to collect Jules's kid from the park and catches a snarky mother's tone when she describes Jules as 'tough', he has her back, pulling the woman into line with a clear-eyed backflip on the word she'd intended as an insult. 'Tough? Sure, she's a total badass. That's how she became an internet sensation. Must make you guys proud, huh? One of your own out there, every day, crashing the glass ceiling of the tech world. So bravo, good for her, huh?' Then he does that 'merrr' Robert De Niro face and leaves the women pickling in their judgemental marinade.

Tough is code, and not a particularly tricky one to crack. Tough, as an adjective for a professional woman, means unappealing, unpleasant, too serious: things women should actively aspire to never be. But when toughness comes parcelled with skill and dedication and a sense of humour, it has the potential to become a less powerful weapon to be wielded against ambitious women. In Jacob Bernstein's 2015 portrait of his late mother, Nora Ephron, the filmmaker and essayist's editor at *The New Yorker* described her using that word, and asserted how beneficial her hardened shell was to her work. 'She was tough,' Robert Gottlieb said. 'Tough is good. Nora would have done nothing had she not been ambitious and she would not have succeeded had she not been tough.' If only all women had someone like Gottlieb to attest to the potential of toughness, instead of the reality most of us are familiar with: that tough = bossy = difficult.

I'm terrified of vocalising my tough-ness. I'm terrified of what someone might say to me, the pressure points they'll know to hit – I've been called a fat cow enough times to know that I can usually expect responses based on how I look, like the real-life versions of those YouTube commenters – if I dare to assert myself, to call someone out for their bad behaviour or speak up against something I know is wrong. My own soft shell prohibits me from doing the things that would allow me to toughen it.

To grow tough, we need to step outside of ourselves and try – something I'm more often than not terrified to do. There is a level of vulnerability in the act of trying that I wasn't prepared to perform for a long time. Australian culture praises sportspeople for training and aspiring, but raises a skeptical eyebrow at the artists and musicians and hopeful tall poppies who peek their ambitious heads above the rest of the bunch. We want to be liked but we can't let anyone know we tried to be.

It's an inherently gendered phenomenon as well; on her presidential campaign trail in 2016, Hillary Clinton was asked by a reporter if she's *too* ambitious; Madonna's work has contributed to culture since the early '80s, but at a certain age her effort was universally declared embarrassing. Women didn't ask to be peddled out like modern freak-show performers but as soon as they succumb to our expectations of their faces and bodies, their plastic surgery decisions are pointed at with the same fingers that prodded and poked at their pre-surgery 'flaws'. We all buy tickets and line up to watch.

One Direction broke the American market like no British pop act did before on the back of their 'we're just a bunch of lads who don't take this too seriously' schtick, meanwhile Little Mix, their female contemporaries from the UK *X Factor* (who actually *won* the competition, where 1D came in third the year before) perform elaborate harmonised vocal runs, spend months rehearsing complex synchronised dances but can't sell the rest of the world on their brand of assertive pro-girl R'n'B.

The young male screenwriters in Hollywood who pen those 'save the cat' narratives are assumed to have the apparent genius required to direct huge features and control gargantuan budgets while wearing schlubby sweatpants, while proven female artists need to squeeze themselves into heels and Spanx to be even considered preliminarily capable to carry a clipboard on that guy's set.

Refusing to try is an understandable response when this is the world you grow up in. During the third season of *Friday Night Lights*, Tyra is attempting to find the morsel of truth buried beneath the dullness of her college application essay. She wrote about her life and job and academic growth and, no matter how honest an account it was, it made for a snoozer of an essay. After some prodding from Landry, she explains why, two years earlier, she had such a dramatic change of heart that spurred her to apply for college in the first place – something she'd never been encouraged to do or told was even an option for her. Before that, she'd never even considered the breadth of her own potential. 'I was afraid of wanting anything,' she confessed to Landry, 'because I was afraid that wanting would lead to trying, and trying would lead to failure. But now I can't stop wanting.' What Tyra is realising here is a universal idea that limits and binds women, and keeps them in place. Trying is embarrassing, because as soon as you do it people know that you care and they can see the vulnerable, fleshy patches of your otherwise hardened shell. It's the reason that effortlessness is just a sought-after vibe. *Get effortless waves!* magazines scream at us, *Don't let him* (it's always 'him') *know you tried, you dumb bitch!* Meanwhile, kids who dare to raise their hands are labelled try-hards and teacher's pets.

Monitoring the ways that women speak and aspire offers up another easy fallback for detractors: if you can't hang shit on what she's saying, pick apart the way she's saying it. It's why *This American Life* listeners are more likely to complain about the vocal fry – the low, apparently very grating register that many people speak in, but that's often attributed to society's most commonly despised and disaffected women, like Britney Spears or the Kardashian sisters – in female presenters' voices than they are to even notice that host Ira Glass has it as well. When men speak and when they write, they do it with the confidence that comes with assuming they're right. Ask any editor: Who is more likely to justify their opinions and who is more likely to protest a rejected pitch? I guarantee they'll tell you the former is women and the latter is men. For women to carry themselves with an air of assumed authority is to put themselves in a position to be struck down and taught a lesson.

One of the first lessons Penny taught me when she became the Jedi Master to my faithful Padawan was the three phrases that women need to memorise in order to be perceived as direct and unemotional in bro-heavy work environments. They are: 'Stop interrupting me', 'I just said that', and 'No explanation needed'. Penny was quoting an article by Soraya L Chemaly that investigates the gender-based divides in speech habits and the ways that men both anecdotally and historically step over women when they're speaking.

When I was working in advertising in my early 20s, I let the men around me take credit for my ideas and palm off their fuck-ups onto me, just as I did with my classmates and project partners in high school and university. Once, I was called in to help brainstorm ideas for a big presentation our agency was pitching to a major bank. It was a huge job and would've been a boon for our small company. The target audience for the campaign was university-age people, as young as eighteen and no older than 25. Also in the room with me were close to a dozen men ranging in age from their late 20s to early 40s. I was the only woman there, and the only person in the demographic we were hoping to appeal to. I summoned the courage to offer feedback on the team's ideas, but the responses I got in return reminded me why women don't do that often. Pointing out that eighteen-year-olds on their first day of university might not enjoy being shot out of a cannon for the sake of a bank's #viral #content earned me nasty looks and the pointed response that changing the idea to satisfy me would sacrifice all that made it edgy. I was told in no uncertain terms that taking my feedback in mind and ensuring the idea was designed to appeal to girls as well as thrill-seeking boys would make it 'light' and 'fluffy'. I left work filled with poorly disguised fury tears that day and told my boss I would be too busy to contribute to the pitch anymore. They presented their ideas without me and didn't win the job. This kind of active dismissal and discouragement of women isn't reserved just for the ad industry – men in all professions create unsupportive or hostile environments by either not including women or by shooting down the ideas they summon the strength to express if they are eventually invited into the room. In the murky grey space between 'good guys' and 'misogynists' are all the men who mightn't say sexist things around women, but who perpetuate this insidious culture that puts women in their place regardless.

What happened in that meeting had also been a theme in my non-work life; feeling insulted or offended made me decide to avoid conversations that could potentially change future interactions. No one at my work apologised after that awful meeting, but if they had I know I would've let them off the hook for the sake of their comfort and so as not to come across as a bitch. Tired of feeling like a pushover when people sought to diminish me, soon after that I made a choice to avoid saying the words 'it's okay' when I didn't mean them. Excusing bad behaviour with those two tiny words has been a common thread in my personal dissatisfaction, and I had realised how effective they were in diluting how I felt for the benefit of whoever made me feel that way. It took time and I was forced to find alternatives, but now, if someone does something that is so fucking not okay, I'm not going to shrug it off by assuring them that there's no harm done. It's a tiny act, but refusing to vocalise this amiability goes a long way in making me feel tough like Nora or self-assured like Miranda.

Now, I make a point to wipe meek modifiers like 'I'm just wondering' from my work emails (a 'just' or two here and there add up to diminish all the work you've done to be in a position to be sending power emails in the first place); I am training myself out of apologising before stating an opinion or fact I know to be true. And I'm not the only one taking these conscious steps to counterbalance performed sweetness. In 2016 I spent three days in Sydney talking to and about creative women at the inaugural Make Nice conference. During a final panel, the conference co-founder Alexandra Winters echoed these sentiments, and declared her own flag-in-the-sand moment where checking her speech had led to a renewed sense of personal power.

Alex had done a master's degree that involved interviewing dozens of people about her area of expertise, one that she'd spent years researching. Despite knowing what she was talking about, Alex realised that she was doing an injustice to her hard-won knowledge by saying 'I guess' before every thought she expressed during interviews. It wasn't until she had to listen to and transcribe every occurrence of it that she realised just how pervasive it was. 'I made a conscious point to stop saying "I guess" when I know my shit,' she told the audience of women in the audience, similarly stuck between the two camps of Confidence and Pleasantness.

I can't help but think that likeability is a trap, not least because wanting to be liked is itself one of the least-likeable traits a woman can display. If you try too hard to be liked, as our girl Anne Hathaway has been wont to do, it has the reverse effect on people; it makes them like you even less. Wanting to be liked, it seems, is almost worse taking the Kristen Stewart route and not giving a shit whether we're liked or not, as long as we're making work that matters to us.

And yet, it doesn't feel fair when these options – to be likeable at the expense of your self-worth, or labelled universally bratty for not changing your attitude to satisfy someone else – render you either *needy* or *difficult*. We can't win. Likeability shouldn't be held up as a goal or achievement, because to reach it we need to sacrifice so much of our determination, ambition and self-esteem.

We're told we need to make ourselves smaller and quieter in order to be liked. But when we do that, who are the people who are going to like us? Before she made *Transparent*, writer and director Jill Soloway was the co-executive producer on the

HBO series *Six Feet Under*, a show that came to define the model of how to craft compelling stories about unlikeable people. According to writer Deborah Goldstein, Soloway asks herself, 'Am I making a cisgender, straight, white man at home feel better? And if I'm not, then the character becomes unlikeable.' With this declaration, Soloway considers the parameters for quote-unquote 'acceptable' human behaviour, knowing that stepping outside of them means offending a portion of the population who'd likely never understand her characters' motivations anyway. I don't know about you, but that's an audience I'm okay with alienating if it's a byproduct of displaying strength, confidence and power. Because the stories of unlikeable women, tough women, difficult women are ones that are worth watching, worth telling and worth living.

CHAPTER 5

REAL QUALITY

I've lost count of the number of times I've been interrogated by 'serious' and 'credible' music makers/writers/listeners because I have spent so much of my time and energy listening to and writing about a boyband. It's happened at parties and events and in my own home and immediately after being introduced by a mutual friend who mentions my dedication to the church of One Direction to the person I'm meeting for the first time. Their confused and skeptical questions run the gamut from, 'Why One Direction?' to, 'How can I take you seriously now?' and are never not dripping in judgement, inferring that either:

a) I'm joking or my obsession is rooted in irony

or

b) there's a rational explanation for liking *anything*, one that goes beyond *I just do* ¯_(ツ)_/¯ .

Early on in my Directionerhood, I went through a phase that had me thinking I'd uncovered something my peers weren't able to appreciate, like I was in on a secret and everyone else's snootiness – about pop music in general and boybands in particular – meant they'd never be privy to the levels of joy it brought me. *Too bad for them! They're just too small-minded to GET IT.* (No, you're not misreading that: my response to being on the receiving end of cultural superiority was to dish it out myself.)

This circle-jerk of taste judgement is endless, like an ouroboros of snark. And it exists everywhere! Every time someone says they like 'all music except rap and country', every time the Greg Daniels adaptation of Ricky Gervais's *The Office* is presumed to be of lower quality purely because it's not the original, every time a baby boomer comments on a post on *Rolling Stone*'s Facebook page about how music died when Jim Morrison did, the garden of the Great Taste Debate is fertilised. We cling to the things that we love because we think they represent who we are, and during that process we forget that we are never stagnant: our bodies are always growing and adapting and so is who we are inside them. I know this for certain because, aside from the baby boomer commenting, I was once guilty of performing all the rockist behaviour I now despise.

I know! What a plot twist!

I can't pinpoint when I developed the now-naive-but-then-very-real idea that the music I listened to reflected my value as a human, but it was somewhere between hanging a portrait of Elvis above my bed as a six year old, and programming my first Nokia phone to play a monophonic version of Simple Plan's 'Addicted' at age thirteen. In that wedge of the pie chart that is my life, buying a Ramones record meant I was more evolved than my Top 40 radio-listening peers, and hiring *The Breakfast Club* from Bundaberg's Blockbuster Video automatically made me smarter and better than anyone who steered themselves towards the new releases. In my Year 10 English class, we were set an assignment that required delivering a persuasive speech about an issue we cared about. My classmates wrote theirs on topics like abortion rights and capital punishment; I tried to argue that 50 Cent represented the decline of quality music, and implored the class to instead listen to the music of John Mayer, someone I saw as being more genuine, more legitimate, and above what I heard being played on the radio at the time.

What I *can* put my finger on is why the work of white male artists was so validated in my mind, and why I thought it acceptable to reject the work of rappers or women singers or groups with predominantly female fan bases: because so much cultural value is rooted in androcentric misogyny and white supremacy. I wanted to be Elvis, not the black artists whose work he aped and then re-sold to white America; when I made my first foray into rap at age twelve, it was via *8 Mile*-era Eminem and a censored version of *The Eminem Show*. I was a white kid consuming the stuff that white kids understood, including the unspoken but assumed opinions that the work of white men was inherently more important than any other. Like so much other information that implanted in my head during that formative time, this was an idea I'd spend years unlearning later on. I bought expensive CD/DVD sets released by emo-punk bands and stayed up late to watch, alone in my lounge room, the videos of white men in bands singing songs about women to rooms of boys who both lusted after the girls in their lives and waited for the opportunity to call them sluts or fakes. (Sometimes they'd be fake sluts – a real two-for-one!) I adoringly memorised lyrics to songs by Taking Back Sunday and Brand New, not sparing a thought for the girl both bands were singing about; the one whose alleged infidelity gave cause for her to be wished to die in various violent (*but poetic*) ways.

The ignorance around my politics of consumption weren't limited to my teenage years. This past year I felt so out of the loop because I had somehow missed the telegram that every twenty-something woman I knew had received with urgency years earlier – the one that read 'WE ALL NEED TO BE READING ELENA FERRANTE'S NEAPOLITAN NOVELS STOP'. But despite being critical successes and immensely popular with every woman on public transport, not even this series of four books was safe from criticism.

In a story on *LA Review of Books*' Avidly channel, Sarah Blackwood and Sarah Mesle wrestle with the clashing ideas that the cover art for Ferrante's bildungsroman series about friends Lenù and Lila growing up and learning about the world was either designed to look cheesy and fluffy (ie like women's fiction) ironically, or that the cringe-inducing artwork was unintentionally so. Unable to agree with either rationale, the Sarahs posit that the cover art is 'straightforward, compelling, and absolutely devastating' and that 'the problem is that we've been trying to reconcile these covers with our taste, and we cannot do that currently, because these covers love women, whereas, as we all know, taste is just another word for internalised misogyny.'

It's so true it almost hurts to realise. We've been suckers for these concepts of -legitimacy- and -taste- our entire lives, without twigging to the fact that all those ideas are doing is giving us convenient excuses to dismantle the work by/about/

for women, people of colour, LGBTQI people and anyone from an historically oppressed group. When the cover of a certifiably brilliant book is decorated to look like something 'for chicks' we feel a little embarrassed, like we're lovingly stirring a pot on the stove and its contents begin spitting at us, potentially hurting us. We resent loving things that make themselves hard to love.

Bundaberg had an independent record store for about two years when I was in high school, right in the place where the Venn diagram of my seminal musical education and peak cultural snobbery intersected. I loved browsing the racks for albums by bands I'd only heard about in alt music magazines or conversations between Lane and her bandmates on *Gilmore Girls*. When other kids my age came in looking for punk music like what they'd heard Lee Harding perform on *Australian Idol*, I'd join in laughing at their expense as I mail-ordered the Ramones poster Seth hung on his bedroom walls in *The OC*, and $40 imported Bright Eyes albums. I wore the mounting debt with pride. I wish, now, that I'd been confident enough to give less of a shit. I wish I'd been a little less desperate to frame myself as a smart outsider who kept a scrapbook of photos of Weezer I'd cut out from copies of *Rolling Stone* to take to the record store so I could remember what colour their album was named after. I wish I gave up on my obsession with Simple Plan – a band I thought I'd discovered because their videos played during the middle of the night on *Rage*, Australia's long-running music video show – purely because I didn't like them anymore, not because I saw their appearance in a Mary-Kate and Ashley movie as them 'selling out'. I wish I didn't silently inflict the same level of scorn on my classmates as *Seinfeld* viewers did on Susan, George's despised girlfriend-turned-fiancée; when George was telling Jerry how much he wanted to watch 'the game' and she called out from the other room, *'I* taped "Mad About You"!', the show told us everything we needed to know about her taste and her value. We all hated her in that moment. I wish, when it came to music, that I could've expanded my idea of 'good' vs 'bad' to take into account things that made me feel something, regardless of the assumed legitimacy they held.

Instead, I spent years (and the money I made at weekend jobs) on records I didn't really enjoy listening to by Australian hardcore bands, because they offered me a sliver of authenticity and the DIY ideology I'd read about in the coffee table books about the history of punk I borrowed from the local library. Bundaberg wasn't exactly a key stop for bands, and so many of the ones that did stop off to play all-ages shows at the PCYC were made up of pierced local boys who all wore one another's band's t-shirts. I went to the shows and took photos of my friends' bands posing in front of poorly graffitied walls and got my lip pierced. I wanted so badly to be unique that I was following in the well-worn path of every poseur teenager who had come before me.

I wasn't just the assumed arbiter of taste, either; part of my attitude came as a response to the raised eyebrows I received when I talked about punk. I committed myself to memorising facts about the Ramones and sought out the one teacher at my school who had seen them in concert in the early '90s to bombard him with questions about what their shows were really like. When my parents separated, my dad would invite me over to watch documentaries like *End of the Century: The Story of the Ramones* when they aired on pay TV. I wanted to be legit and I wanted to stuff my pockets with trivia and information so I could easily whip it out to prove my worth if called upon. Which happened sooner than I thought. The first time I debuted the 'Beat on the Brat' t-shirt I'd set up an eBay account to buy, I was stopped by a man who wore sunglasses indoors as he scoffed, 'You're a fan of the Ramones, are you?' I had been so proud that my shirt's pre-faded screenprint made it look like it was less than brand new and didn't expect a Sunday church service – where I was at the time – to be the place where I'd be demoted to a fake. 'I am!' I told him proudly. Without missing a beat, he said, 'If you love them so much, tell me how many chords they played.'

I was shocked at how quickly all my love and research was annihilated, and mad at myself for not having *that* answer handy. I didn't know the answer then. I still don't; I couldn't care less how many chords a guitarist plays if they're making music that connects with something inside me or bringing characters like Riff Randell, the heroine in the Ramones' fictional concert film *Rock'n'Roll High School*, into my life.

When I was seventeen, a new girl arrived at my school and was placed in the same film and television class I had been taking for a few years. One day, while sharing screenplays we had written, our teacher was questioning a very specific prop the new girl had incorporated into her story: a 'hand chair'. I sat at the back of the room watching her struggle to describe what the piece of furniture was and how it connected to her screenplay, before getting a little spark of recognition.

'Do you mean like the one in *Arrested Development*?' I asked her, remembering how the character Buster had one in his room as a background prop that became a permanent joke set-up after his own hand was bitten off by a seal.

The new girl's eyes lit up. 'Yes!' she cried, 'You know *Arrested Development*? I love you!' Basing a friendship on the cult TV show today would mean you'd have too many friends for Facebook to handle, but keep in mind that this was 2007, in a very small town in regional Australia, at a school where I regularly spent entire recesses explaining to my classmates who 'Tom from Myspace' was, and why they were friends with him as soon as they made a profile, and why, no, he won't give you some of the money he made from selling the website. There wasn't a whole lot happening in our cultural landscape, so of course it seemed valid for a vulnerable new student arriving at a new school – one that she was about to graduate from – to attempt to forge a connection based on a semi-obscure American comedy and nothing else. For weeks afterwards, until she fell in with a crowd she related to on less of a surface level, she'd follow me into class so we could sit together, and coincidentally line up right behind me at the tuckshop during lunch.

What she did in those weeks was what I had spent (and would continue to spend) years doing: confusing what somebody liked for who they are. I iced out women who spent money to see the Black Eyed Peas in concert, and gave too much credit to boys whose iTunes libraries were filled with songs by bands whose names I didn't recognise. I was Lane Kim, listing my musical influences alphabetically, worshipping at the altar of CBGB and looking down on anyone who didn't know that Kim Deal was in both the Breeders *and* the Pixies. I'm 26 now and, when I hear people talking about the Replacements with encyclopaedic knowledge, I still get a tremor of recognition that tells me: *this person is cool.* That feeling of not knowing something I innately can tell that I *should* know is a motivator; it makes me want to keep learning until I know. For a long time, that feeling told me all I needed to know about a person's value.

Only with hindsight can I identify the passive misogyny I employed to drag down women for their musical preferences while I put men on pedestals for theirs. You can bet that if a girl I didn't know or like talked about my favourite bands I'd find an excuse to label her fandom inauthentic. If a guy I thought was cool said he liked a Top 40 pop song, I'd find a way to incorporate it into a playlist and question myself for being unable to see the worth that only his brilliant male mind could appreciate.

Our tastes may not reflect who we are, but they certainly have an effect on how people perceive us. This is something Hillary Clinton learned for damn sure while campaigning for president in 2016. While contesting the democratic ticket against Senator Bernie Sanders, Senator Clinton became the subject of a meme that equated her apparent desperation for the position with both her lack of credibility as a cultural tastemaker and her eagerness to please. It took the form of a poster with both of their smiling faces on it. 'Be informed. Compare them on the issues that matter' the headline read, and each incarnation of the meme involved a different pop culture artefact that the characters of 'Bernie' and 'Hillary' would share their thoughts on. Sanders's made-up responses were always in depth and tapped into opinions shared by respected critics and devoted fans. Clinton's were cloying or obvious, and displayed points of view held by the masses, ie idiots, ie women.

In a piece for *Salon* called 'Bernie bros, stop this meme: Your dumb joke about Hillary's music taste isn't funny – it's predictably sexist', Annie Zaleski took the trend to task by rightfully comparing it to an often anti-woman or anti-pop sentiment that abounds in music criticism. 'The meme's subtext has uncomfortable parallels to the authenticity wars that continue to rage in rock circles, the idea that certain acts and genres are more real because they don't employ an army of songwriters or laptops,' she said. Zaleski goes on to lay out the myriad ways that pervasive gender bias elevates men for interests or behaviours that women would be chastised for displaying. There were so many points on which to compare Sanders and Clinton that the way the latter's female-ness correlated with her cool factor (or lack thereof) needn't have played a role.

But this is not an ideal world where that kind of reasoned thinking takes place. If it were, I likely wouldn't have convinced myteenself that going to see garbage local punk and hardcore bands I pretended to like was an appropriate and validating way to spend my time. I wouldn't have sacrificed so much of myself to win favour with boys who said they *just didn't think women can be good musicians*. I mourn the time I spent clinging to these militant but misguided ideas about legitimacy, while forcing myself to find value in music or films, TV shows or books I didn't respond to because I was told they were the ones I *should* like. All that time spent trying to connect with *Fight Club* or Sonic Youth could've been much better spent listening to Janet Jackson or watching *Degrassi* – pop culture artefacts I had to retroactively catch up to.

I shared a bond with one of my high school teachers not unlike the one Eli Cash had with Etheline in *The Royal Tenenbaums*; I sought his approval and respected him as a human as much as I did as an educator. He wasn't the kind of young teacher, fresh out of university, who gave me a desire to re-enact an

'O Captain! My Captain!' moment. He never perched on the edge of a desk or insisted we call him by his first name. He was middle-aged and greying with a wife and kids, and he sometimes came back from lunch smelling faintly like the cigarettes we all knew the teachers smoked in their cars before the bell rang.

I wanted him to think I was smart and cool because he was smarter than anyone I'd ever met and recognised the words I'd scrawled on my Year 10 pencil case as Modest Mouse lyrics. Soon after that, he burned me a copy of the Shins' debut record, *Oh, Inverted World*. He nodded approvingly at the Ramones pins I crammed onto the collar of my shirt and wanted to know what I thought about books and music. Once, I walked past him and two of my other beloved teachers locked in a debate over whether *Yellow Submarine* or *Sgt. Pepper's Lonely Hearts Club Band* was the better Beatles album. He asked my opinion and seemed impressed at my reasoning. (*Sgt. Pepper's*, because *Yellow Submarine* was technically a soundtrack. And also because of 'She's Leaving Home', duh.) After I moved away for university, I kept in touch with him a little with a handful of letters, emails and mixed CDs, silently hoping he'd respect me because of my decision to include a song by a little-known Melbourne band called the Greasers after one by Beck.

He was one of the first people I knew who placed an importance on looking ahead in music; I'm sure he was reading early Pitchfork or other music blogs when I wasn't even aware that a blog was something that could exist outside of Myspace. On my way into his history class one day, he passed me a copy of the first Band of Horses record and wanted my opinion on whether they were a genuinely new band, or just the Shins masquerading as something new to weed out the people who just thought it was cool to like the Shins because they were *the Shins*. I had been so busy, up until that point, diving into the past, trying to consume and archive information about every artist that *Rolling Stone* said had made important records before I was born, that I'd failed to look ahead. So sure that anything made by 'my generation' was, by default, soulless trash passed off as something shiny and fresh, I had fallen behind and out of the loop. One of the greatest joys I've found in being a fan of artists such as One Direction and Kanye West is the thrill of loving in real-time; for once I'm not diving into biographies and forums to find information I was too young to witness for myself. Instead, I can track the updates on *The Life of Pablo* as they happen; I can follow intimately the changing setlists on a global One Direction tour and watch the world react to the artistic and musical importance of a new Beyoncé visual album drop. Forcing myself to be present meant accepting the potential value in new nuggets of culture, which I'd always unquestioningly assigned to White Man's Work that had been created before I was.

Before I discovered the bone-deep joy that came from watching every episode of *Keeping Up With the Kardashians* or re-reading the *Sisterhood of the Travelling Pants* series every summer without feeling like I *should've* been reading something boring and dense (ie important) instead, I was operating under the false assumption that I needed to have more than affection for something for it to be worth my time. *I like this* was never enough criteria against which to measure something. It needed to teach me something or challenge me; maybe consuming it needed to be a largely unpleasant experience for it to be worth my time. It had to be something I was proud enough to attach

NO WAY! OKAY, FINE.

to the top of my Myspace interests list or debate over in grim chat rooms where I could wear the points I'd won like a medal on my chest.

So much of the superiority that comes with an appreciation for something obscure/alternative/underground is the difficulty in accessing it: if you can't hear a band on the radio every other hour; if a supermarket or chain record store doesn't sell their CDs; if their name doesn't trigger any recognition in your friends, you feel like you've tapped into something special and deserve a prize for the effort you've invested. You feel like one of few people paying attention, and thrive off that uniqueness until it forms a crucial part of your identity and how you want people to perceive you. Compare that with the saturation and ubiquity of major-label bands whose faces are plastered on everything from billboards to lunchboxes, the ones whose music is shoved down your throat with seemingly no effort or taste barrier required. But there is an entitlement and safety in the assumption that fighting for your entertainment makes you somehow a better person. It's not a coincidence that musical entitlement, in particular, is massively male-dominated and expresses itself in dark clubs where elbows and boots and fists elevate your status and propel you – literally – to the top or the front. Men show their love (of each other, of art) through the violence that forces so many girls and marginalised people to the sidelines. The ones who do summon the strength to enter these spaces are assumed to be there for the 'wrong' reasons – the singer is cute or the merch is cool or the boy with great hair at school scribbles the band's logo on his Chuck Taylors. Those girls can't possibly appreciate music in the same way the boys do – all boots and fists and barely repressed aggression. Those things combine to create unquestioned credibility.

Comparatively, pop concerts and fan networks are welcoming; the lights are on and everybody's contributions are valued. Even if what you have to say has been said before, it only reinforces the idea of connection and belonging. Fan-built spaces are essential for all people, but especially for girls, because they offer clearly marked entry points that, once inside, nurture community and critical listening. The image of fangirls who only want to scream at the tinted windows of vans and pash the floppy-haired singer devalue the nuanced discussions about lyrics and album art that girls would love to have everywhere if they were guaranteed not to be called dumb whores for speaking their mind. Pop music, reality TV and, now for girls a few years younger than me, YouTube channels, are accessible; you don't need to pass some arbitrary quiz about chord progressions to earn your fandom here, and you aren't devalued as being 'just' a girl at a punk show, someone who's only there to pick up dudes who've spent too long listening to Blink-182 songs about girls falling in love from the crowd.

Once I finally became mildly okay with sharing my less-punk, less-intellectual interests with the world, anything I loved but was unable to intellectualise was given a new name: guilty pleasure. I might have spent years obsessively searching on Kazaa for every song ever played on *The OC* (and crying for hours when its fourth season finale aired), but it was a *teen drama*, which meant it was relegated to the guilty pleasure bin until nostalgic internet articles assured me my fandom was objectively okay. Madeleine Davies's essay for *Jezebel* on this topic summarises the inherent self-criticism of 'guilty pleasures' in its title alone:

'"Hate Watching" is Mostly Just Being Embarrassed by our Own Tastes'.

'For some reason, we often feel the need to cloak our broader tastes in a layer of irony,' she writes. 'We use terms like *hate-watch* and *guilty pleasure* so we don't have to admit that Honey Boo Boo makes us laugh or that we cried during every episode of *Grey's Anatomy*.' I identified so much with the crisis of taste and guilt she presented that I had to confront in myself the contradiction at play in my consumption habits. It was as if the good taste required to avoid these shows and movies and bands weren't enough to earn haughty bragging rights; I also tricked myself into believing that I needed to possess the good taste and self-awareness it required to watch them anyway *but not really enjoy it*. Someone asked me recently how I find the time to watch as much TV as I do, and I couldn't come up with a response that didn't make me sound like I'm a lonely and brain-dead hermit for not only choosing to spend so much of my life in front of a screen, but for queuing up so much vapid reality TV on it. We make choices about how we spend our time and, since that's such a valuable and limited commodity, we're supposed to spend it 'well', make the *right* choices. We're meant to only spend our time watching and thinking about the things that we all agree are the best and important things to watch and think about.

I say fuck that.

I'm going to list now the TV shows I haven't spent my time consuming but, by all accounts – and according to the men who get into loud conversations about them in my general vicinity – I 'should have' seen: *The Wire, The Sopranos, Breaking Bad, Dexter, House of Cards, The Walking Dead, The Americans, The*

West Wing, Boardwalk Empire, Masters of Sex, The Newsroom, The Affair, Sons of Anarchy, Scandal, Lost. (I know it's risky putting this information here – *Can you believe you're reading a book written by someone who hasn't watched a white guy do crimes but also be loved and admired?! How can you trust me?!*)

It's not because there are too many shows to keep up with, nor is it because I'm ~too busy~ to spend time with these shows. I set aside days to catch up on literal hours of *Jane the Virgin*, have cycled through every season of *America's Next Top Model* and *The Real Housewives of Melbourne*; I've spent an estimated seven trillion hours of my life watching Lorelai and Rory Gilmore embark on coffee-soaked walk-and-talks around Stars Hollow; I grieve for the prematurely cancelled NBC sitcom *Best Friends Forever*, that ran for just two months/six episodes in 2012, and have re-watched it countless times in the years since.

If anything, the combined effects of my limited capacity to spend time with new pieces of culture – in this example it's TV shows but the same rules also apply to movies and music – and the fact that I know I cannot watch it all, result in me narrowing down the things I feel content to dedicate myself to. There is an agreement in place when I press play, an exchange of emotion that decrees that the time I spend with a show or movie or band will cause me to Feel A Thing. That's the basis of my commitment now, and it's serving me well. In an episode of his *Game of Thrones* recap show *After the Thrones*, self-described 'recovering TV critic' Andy Greenwald explains that people would often ask him how they should spend their time as a consumer, as though all we invest in television is an allotment of time. 'The truth is,' he explained to co-host Chris Ryan, 'it's a matter of emotional investment; we put a certain amount of ourselves into these shows, into these characters . . . And we trust it; we hope there will be some payoff, that we will have some richness to reward us for the time we spent with these people.' The richness that Greenwald mentions is commonly reaped in the form of social benefits – you can join in the water cooler conversation about a new HBO drama – or an elevation in reputation – you become known as the person with all the most timely opinions on critically acclaimed TV. But there is still a hierarchy of taste at play here; for all the satisfaction we got seeing rockists with their tails between their legs at realising that Taylor Swift's *1989* and Carly Rae Jepsen's *Emotion* deserved serious and thoughtful listening, nobody is seeking out deep readings on *Home and Away*, no matter how much people enjoy it. In some ways, finding peace with the cultural products I consume despite their absence from Best Of lists means coming to terms with the fact that I'll likely always need to be able to defend the time and emotional investments I make in them.

I'll happily watch *Here Comes Honey Boo Boo* from start to finish, the voice of my nineteen-year-old self who was desperate to be the kind of person who could effortlessly drop a reference to Jean-Luc Godard into conversation becoming just a whisper in the back of my mind, drowned out by Alana screaming at her pet pig. Because I like these things. They make me feel true joy and connection. And sometimes that's enough. The cheesiest TV show with the broadest appeal and lowest bar for laughs can still make me cry. And a band of boys who tumble around on stage and sing about going to bed with a cup of tea can still have as great an impact as if it were a wise man with a guitar whose work had been pre-approved by the wise council of Men With Opinions.

I don't think it's a coincidence that my rejection of the concept of guilty pleasures coincided with my discovery of One Direction – a band *so* worthy of the 'guilty' marker they not only make formulaic pop music marketed primarily towards teenage girls, but they started doing it on a *reality TV singing competition*. I was resistant at first: everything these floppy-haired teenagers represented was everything I'd battled against for so long. I thought they were too pretty to possibly make any good music, too young to make anything I'd like, too popular to ever make a dint on any valuable level. But they did more than make a dint; they drove headlong into my taste centre and changed the way it worked.

That change came slowly, then all at once. A passing amusement at their 2011 *Saturday Night Live* appearance turned into a plea to my friend Hannah (an early fan) for a guide to the key videos and articles I needed to consume in order to *get* the band and, perhaps most importantly, to understand the in-jokes about them I'd noticed were proliferating on Tumblr. Before this discovery, I'd chastised the fans who'd bought tickets to see the band in concert a full sixteen months before their 2013 tour came to Australia – this passing pop trend couldn't possibly last that long! By the time that tour came around I was desperately scouring the internet for dodgy resale tickets, so essential it was that I see the objects of my newfound affection and obsession in the flesh.

I eventually got to see them twice on that tour, and from the moment I entered the Melbourne arena for the first time, I felt a connection to every single other body in the room. Girls outside stood pressed against the doors clutching signs that said 'WE DON'T HAVE TICKETS BUT WE CAME TO

SUPPORT YOU'; inside, the similarly decorated placards read 'YOU'RE OUR IDOLS' or 'YOU SAVED MY LIFE'. With One Direction, I got to relive the joy of being a young music fan without the shame or posturing that were ubiquitous during my own teen years. The coolness, aggression or ambivalence that alternated in my experiences in punk were nonexistent here; there was no distance or violence between the tens of thousands of fans exchanging phone numbers and holding hands when they excitedly took their seats. I was so proud to be among them.

We all collectively anticipated the key moments in the show we knew were coming because we'd memorised every moment of every previous show thanks to our online community of fan archivists. Rather than spoiling what was to come, knowing the ins and outs of the show only made the anticipation more delicious; knowing what was *supposed* to happen on the almost-identical shows meant we knew when we saw something improvised or when the band performed a short preview of a track from their as-yet-unreleased album (something that happened at one of my shows! I know, I am *so* lucky). Those moments were history-making, and being a part of them felt incredible.

Eventually, my love of One Direction and my then-simmering writing career merged and the band became my beat. I wrote essays about discovering them and about the heaving piles of disregard dumped upon their savvy fans. I presented a paper on them at an academic music conference with Greil Marcus, Jessica Hopper, Charles Aaron, Laura Snapes and other critics I admire in the audience. I was called for comment the day Zayn Malik left the band, and approached with assignments from my favourite music publications when the band's first Zayn-free album was due to be released. Rather than destroying my reputation as a pop culture writer, my love for this band only fed it. As my writing (hopefully) legitimised elements of the band that had been disregarded as mainstream pop fluff, so too was my career legitimised because of my vocal interest in them. Loving One Direction proudly and publicly as an adult is significant because it's important for young girls to see that growing older doesn't mean giving up your affection. You don't have to abandon your adoration just because you start paying tax.

My affection for them is hard to explain and justify, which is what convinced me of its purity. This love wasn't ironic or tinged with guilt or the result of an academic study; it was whole and true and validating, and taught me that the same love could be felt for other pieces of what I would have once rejected as cultural detritus. If I could let myself love One Direction without shame, I could lower my shield of legitimacy and accept that I didn't have to fight battles on behalf of the Taste Police anymore.

CHAPTER 6

DEAR EVERY FRIEND I'VE EVER BROKEN UP WITH

We barely even knew that was happening, did we? Dang. One day you're sleeping head-to-toe in my tiny bed, the next Facebook has started to filter your posts out of my feed based on its hectic algorithm that tells them how infrequently we interact now. You went from dominating my social life and text message history to sending 'new phone who dis' when I invited you out. A lot happened in between, I know, and neither of us was to blame, I suppose. My instinct tells me I should feel more sad about how it all turned out than I do, but the truth is neither of us was prepared to strap up our wrists and fight for it.

It wasn't often a conscious decision (except for those times when it was); it might've started with a gradual falling-out-of-touch where we only checked in on each other when we were both back in our hometown at Christmas, or maybe we started avoiding each other at parties after silently and mutually agreeing that the most recent nail in the coffin would be the final one.

It might've ended because the boyfriend or girlfriend or room-mate or band or bar that was the connecting force between us stopped being part of one of our lives. One of us broke up with that boyfriend or girlfriend or moved away from that sharehouse or bar or stopped listening to the same bands. There just wasn't a place to meet in the middle anymore. You know, no hard feelings.

Now I just like the photos you post to Facebook from the wedding you had, surrounded by friends I don't know, and the subsequent honeymoon you went on with someone I've never met. Not even the deepest dive into your Instagram feed, performed when I'm wearing pimple cream and should've been asleep hours earlier, can fill me in on the details of your life and relationship that, someday, I would've known.

I don't think I was ever truly honest with you, and that's a big reason why it couldn't work. You weren't to know about those times I heard someone at school mention a party, decided that overhearing counted as an invitation and went along myself, uninvited and unprepared for the loneliness that comes with having no fun in a place where everyone else appears to be. (That is, when I was brave enough to get out of my mum's car in the first place. More than once she drove me to a party and, only when we arrived did we both realise no one had replied to my pleas to meet me there so I didn't have to walk through the doors alone, and we turned around and drove home, where I half-scrubbed my glittering eyeshadow off and pulled on my pyjamas.)

You might not have realised how much power you had in our friendship, how desperate I was to disguise myself as a person you'd want to know and be seen with. Or maybe you did. Maybe you were one of the many who kept me close to make yourself feel a little better. I don't think you knew exactly what you were doing as you were doing it – I certainly didn't. I don't think you were really vindictive enough to talk about your extensive list of body goals that, when achieved, would mean you were no longer 'a fat piece of shit' (your words), not considering the fact that you were literally half my physical size at the time. You were talking about yourself, but not really.

Maybe I'm not giving you enough credit. Maybe you didn't mean to embarrass me when you asked loudly if I was a virgin in front of a group, including a boy I'd told you I liked. And I like to hold out hope that you forgot I'd told you about that crush when you instructed me to sleep on the couch after a party because you'd set that same guy up with your best friend and they were together in the bed I was meant to sleep in, in the room where my overnight bag and toothbrush and clean underwear were stowed away in the cupboard. Maybe you didn't know I'd find out that you had two birthday parties that year: one that I was invited to, and one that was designed for the sole purpose of talking about me when I wasn't around.

Maybe I took it too hard when you said or did something that hurt, maybe you didn't mean it, maybe I shouldn't have expected you to stick up for me when people called me names or threw things. Maybe it was wrong and petty of me to cata-logue every unkind thing you said or ignored, to keep a tally and carry that collection of wrongdoings with me. Maybe I was the one who sabotaged our friendship from the moment it began, when I walked in with that now-heaving bag slung over my shoulder, and refused to throw it in the bin. I carry the baggage of hurt and resentment from one friendship to the next, unpacking only the essentials and accumulating excess charges every time I depart again.

My diaries from my late teens are testament to my inability to summon the words to really explain how I feel to you, the person who has any power to change a situation. It's there, in those private pages, where I write the things I really want to say to you, divulging the feelings I've kept bottled up for months.

'I was tempted to write a letter, but that seemed a little dramatic. Plus, it could so easily be misinterpreted,' I reason with myself. *'I resent you for wanting to spend more time with your new boyfriend than you do with me, and I resent you for remembering I'm there when he goes on tour with his band or on a weekend away with his mates. And I resent myself for still being there when you turn around and remember how you needed me once.*

'It would be so easy to just stay home, save money and give people a chance to miss me,' I write to an audience of only myself, *'but I'm likely to get cabin fever in a few days and, when I finally get out of the house, what if nobody's missed me or noticed I've been gone?'*

During the time we spent together, you were like the doctor I made an emergency appointment with when I first had an infected Bartholin's gland cyst (don't google it unless u nasty): you saw a very small part of me but we didn't spend enough time together for you to really know me. It's no wonder we didn't last. I couldn't always see myself clearly because my vision was clouded with what you wanted me to be. Every day I'm still trying to find my truth while simultaneously trying so hard not to cringe at that phrase; every day I'm trying to honestly answer the questions: Who are you? What are you good at? What makes you happy? In the hope that I can tap into the little nuggets I'd honestly rather avoid because vulnerability is scary as shit. That hesitation might have ruined any potential we had.

Maybe I felt forgotten about, like Sasha does in the movie *Life Partners*, when her best friend, Paige, dates then moves in with then gets engaged to a guy called Tim, while Sasha's still navigating the dating scene and the concept of holding down a job. When Paige says Sasha should've known one of them would become unavailable when they settled down with someone, and that it's not fair to expect her attention every day and night anymore, Sasha counters by reminding Paige that she still has someone to talk to all night, it's just that it's Tim now. Sasha wants Paige to acknowledge the gap in her life that she once filled, and the fact that Paige doesn't have a similar empty space.

Maybe I saw myself in that. Maybe when you hurt me I said 'it's fine' and 'that's okay' when I really should've taken a leaf out of Sasha's book and verbalised how I felt, whether that was saying, 'I'm mad about this' or 'I'm lonely' or 'I feel like you're forgetting me and that makes me act like a passive-aggressive bitch and I'm sorry for *that* but we still need to have a discussion.'

I'm not a victim; I know I played a role in our dissolution. In one page of my teenage diary I spelled all the hopes I had for the rest of my life, including a list of all the relationships I wanted to preserve. Looking at the names on that list, so many of which belong to people I haven't spoken to since the year I archived them on a page, I can see the common thread between them all is me. That page is like a cemetery of lost relationships I didn't try to save.

DEAR EVERY FRIEND I'VE EVER BROKEN UP WITH

Maybe I was drawn to you because of the ways in which we were similar, but I grew to hate the parts of you that reminded me of myself and rather than confronting those weaknesses in myself I blamed you for sharing them.

I've never been good at keeping secrets because passing them on makes me seem complex and interesting; I was always quick to jump on the defensive, to protect my own feelings and sacrifice yours, to whip out my go-to comeback from *Romy and Michele's High School Reunion* ('You're a bad person with an ugly heart, and we don't give a flying fuck what you think!') over MSN Messenger to make it seem like I didn't care when I really deeply did; and I relied on passive-aggression for a long time because it seemed easier to let resentment pile up like a petty Jenga tower than it was to just give you an FYI on my feelings.

Remember that episode of *Gilmore Girls* when Rory sees a group of cheerleaders from Stars Hollow High School and realises her best friend, Lane, is among them? And she feels kind of rattled and off-kilter because her lifelong friend has gone from plotting a complete personal archive of every album mentioned in *The Mojo Collection: The Ultimate Music Companion* and making fun of the popular cheerleaders (Rory and Lane are cool and smart, you know, so that means they think all upbeat blonde girls are dumb-dumbs) to becoming one of them. More than that, though, is the fact that Lane changed while Rory's back was turned. When we don't see each other for weeks or years at a time, I return as an increasingly involved/evolved version of myself, but I recognise in Rory that sense of betrayal at the reality of how much you (and Lane) have also changed in the meantime. I need to remind myself that people aren't permanent, that your brain and heart are shifting and adjusting just like mine are.

I mightn't have been able to communicate well enough then to get you to fully understand how invested I was, or how much it hurt to know it was over. When Eric visits Susan's big, empty apartment in the movie *Girlfriends* and asks why she left his house after they first slept together, and she tells him she had just come out of a long relationship, he didn't know it had been with her best friend, Anne, who got married and moved out. But you and I know that's how it feels; we know what it's like to be that deep with someone, before the plug is suddenly yanked out. We know that the end of a platonic friendship shouldn't hurt the way any other kind of love hurts when it's surgically removed, but it does, even if it's not supposed to.

You didn't know this at the time – and, truthfully, neither did I – but you were a very special piece in the puzzle I was building for a very specific life I thought I was supposed to want to have. I wanted to have a youth worth writing about and reminiscing over, one that I could revisit and reference in films or stories. I wanted to have so many experiences with you that I might start to forget some, and years later only a certain song or smell would bring the memory back. I tried on different personas as a kid, and tried on the friends that went with them, all in attempts to one day, hopefully, settle on the ones who suited me best.

As I look back on these relationships that are now very firmly in the past tense, I realise that, without trying to, I've stopped sweating it out in *So You Think You Can Dance: Friendship Edition*. I'm no longer dancing for my life, trying to get a high score, trying to be the person someone else needs me to be to serve their image of themselves, trying and failing to consistently use dancing as a metaphor. I see a tea towel on Etsy that says, 'The best way to appreciate someone is to imagine your life without them.' I will never buy it, but its cloying message helps me realise I've been undertaking a passive and mostly accidental human version of the KonMari method: if anyone in my life or phone contacts or Facebook friends list doesn't bring me joy, I don't put them back on my shelf or in my drawers. I do as Marie Kondo advises, and silently thank them for what they brought to me, before letting them go, trusting they need to find a new person to belong to.

We didn't end on bad terms, but we just stopped bringing each other joy. Like Kanye West says in his advice book *Thank You and You're Welcome*, extracting your life from the loved ones who bring negativity into it is difficult, but essential. He says that knowing you're the best means you need to surround yourself with the same. I might not have the same level of all-caps love for myself yet, but with Kanye's help, in his role as my invisible guardian angel, I can remind myself not to make exceptions.

Before we sit down to eat burgers and watch *Game of Thrones*, Penny shows me a video that illustrates how big the moons and planets are, and it makes me feel queasy. The vastness of the universe is overwhelming when it's just a faraway concept, let alone when you're watching these humungous objects slingshotting towards, then away from, the screen. She tells me about space-time, about the idea that space is three dimensions (*got it*) and time is the fourth (*what?*). I struggle to understand the proposition that *my now* and *her now* and *someone else's now* are all *different nows*, because of the way we are each moving through space-time, jostling against each other and pinging back and forth through space, as time shifts around us. I've always wanted to be able to travel through time, to go back and ctrl+Z stupid things I've said or reactive responses I've had. Maybe if I were an external being – a god or alien or Ed Harris-style director of *The Truman Show* of my life – I could look back at all four dimensions and see where it all changed between us, and fix it. Maybe I'd see that it was worth fixing, or maybe I'd realise we're best the way we are now. If I could see all of time, instead of just the string of *nows* that we live in, I could see the moment we made the decisions that led to the fact that we don't talk anymore.

We're all different now and we'll keep being different. Maybe we'll get to a point where we both become so different that we wind up being the same again. But if that doesn't happen, I think we'll still manage to be okay too.

CHAPTER 7

A HARD PLACE

There are no fewer than four essay collections on my bookshelf filled with writers' stories of moving to, and then away from, New York City. I've read dozens more online, and watched a handful of movies in which dejected young rejects of the five boroughs, the stars that once lit up their eyes noticeably duller now, try to find a home in a new place that can never possibly compare. It seems that the only bigger platitude than being a writer trying to make it in the city is being one who writes about leaving it behind in the rearview mirror. It's a well-worn topic, one that's verging on cliché at this point. Here's my unnecessary contribution to the canon.

It might be that no other place in the world is imbued with as much mystique and inherent pressure as New York City. The tale of people reaching their creative or personal or professional ceilings all over the world and trading in those lives for ones in New York City is as old as the expression 'a tale as old as time'. New York exists in our imaginations even if we've never been there or met anyone who has; it's such an integral part of pop culture and news and history that it's impossible to pinpoint when I became aware of it – as a literal place or just as an idea.

Living there was never something I dreamed of or aspired to. I don't think I did, anyway, although it's hard to know for sure because it seems like something everyone *should* want. But when the opportunity came up – a year into my part-time job as the editor of a culture website in Australia, less than six months after graduating from university – to transfer to the company's Manhattan office, the answer was obvious and immediate. I had to apply for a passport before giving my official answer, and by the time I moved to the other side of the world when I was 21, it had just one stamp in it.

I packed up my sharehouse and said goodbye to my friends and housemate, Steve, in Melbourne. On the plane to my hometown, where I'd spend a few days with my family before flying to Sydney then Los Angeles then New York, I read over and over the card Steve had given me at the airport. He'd driven me there, and my friend Patsy had met us before my flight. Before that day, no one had gone through the rigmarole of airport security just to be able to spend a little extra time with me before I flew away. I couldn't – and still can't – wrap my head around the fact that two people had paid for airport parking just to hug me goodbye.

In the card, Steve described how proud he was of me, and how he knew I'd do great things, that he'd just had a conversation to that effect with our friend Jim, who'd become like a brother to me since I'd moved to Melbourne a few years earlier. Reading it felt like eavesdropping on the nicest eulogy ever; the impulse people have to fake their death just to hear what people say about them at their funeral (a very casual and not-weird daydream I have often) wouldn't exist if we could all read a card like that. I clutched it tightly as the plane taxied out of Tullamarine Airport, and then tucked it safely in the pocket of the seat in front, crying silently as Melbourne fell away underneath me for what I imagined would be the last time.

When I arrived at my mum's house that night, I was exhausted from travel and tears. I went to pull out the card to show her, but it wasn't there. I'd left it in that fucking pocket on the plane. I burst into a fresh round of heaving sobs when I realised that I'd left both my found family and their sentiments behind. My cat, who had been living with my mum since I left for university, had never been affectionate. She'd spent four years running away from our eager hands. But she leapt on my lap that night, nuzzling my legs as I cried into her fur, keeping guard over me as I hung out in the limbo between having said goodbye to one family, and preparing to say goodbye to another.

I arrived in New York in the middle of summer 2011, with nothing. (Not because of some *-three bucks, two bags, one me-* type romanticism, but because Qantas had left my suitcases behind in Sydney.) I was excited to be in a shoddy Airbnb in Williamsburg, impatient for my best friend Anton – who'd found out he was accepted into NYU's Screenwriting Masters program just three days after I found out I'd be moving – to arrive, and terrified of what I'd gotten myself into. I spent my first days ticking things off a list of NYC dreams I never actually bothered to write: taking the subway into Manhattan for the first time; leaving a tip for a bartender with a dollar bill;

ordering a burger to my desired done-ness; seeing a show at Upright Citizens Brigade Theatre; drinking my body weight in iced coffees; getting crippling blisters and shin splints from walking all day in bad shoes; not freaking out when I saw Lesley Arfin *and* Matt and Kim on the same block on the same day.

I had just the weekend to get my bearings in the city before I started running the site full-time, and despite not doing anything wild or outrageous, every tiny thing felt exaggerated because of where it was happening. That scene at the start of *The Hours* when Meryl Streep sasses her florist for not knowing what a poetry prize is, then carries her lilies and roses home, is emblematic of how romantic daily tasks can be purely because they're being performed in the city. The cobblestones beneath her feet seem magical, as did every cramped subway ride I took. Clutching a sweating iced coffee in one hand and a heaving bag of bagels, lox and cream cheese in the other had me imagining I was a background extra in a Whit Stillman movie; seeing the corner of Bowery and Bleecker, once the home of punk mecca CBGB and the place immortalised in my favourite Ramones poster, existed in real life and I could go there to lean against the same lamp pole as Dee Dee Ramone did.

Seth Meyers was born in the Midwest and grew up in New Hampshire, but knew all too well the draw of New York City. In a retrospective for *SNL*, where he was head writer from 2006 to 2014, Seth described how exhilarating it was to stay up watching the show and hearing the cast make jokes that referenced the city's affectations. Relocating there meant being in on the joke. There was a power in *getting it*. You don't really understand John Mulaney's stand-up joke about how the seconds before you die are likely the same as the exact moment of realising you're about to be pummelled by the noise of a Mariachi band on the subway until you hear those joyous yells and guitars as the doors of the train slide closed. Until you entertain out-of-towners who only want to visit Magnolia Bakery and the steaming pit of hell that is Times Square, you can't really get that episode of *Broad City* where Abbi and Ilana pursue across the city the tourist who accidentally stole Abbi's phone. There are no comparisons to the city's particulars anywhere else in the world.

In no other place would Natasha Lyonne and Chloë Sevigny snatch the last two seats at a *Saturday Night Live* taping from you after you waited in line all night outside Rockefeller Plaza. Where else could you go to see Bright Eyes play by the East River and come home to discover your new roommate is Conor Oberst's old friend and gives you his AAA pass from the show to keep as a souvenir? Nowhere else would you have to skip across the street to avoid a homophobic Westboro Baptist Church protest on your way to cover a Fashion Week event at Lincoln Center and bump into Bill Cunningham in his trademark blue jacket as a result. I got to touch those dresses that Rodarte designed to look like van Gogh's *Starry Night*; I saw Peaches cut in the line for a Raincoats reunion show, then took the same route on my walk home as Tobi Vail. I muscled my way into Webster Hall to see Wild Flag play during their brief spark of existence, and saw the cast of *The Royal Tenenbaums* reunite for the film's tenth anniversary. But I squeezed it all in, like Ponyboy in *The Outsiders*, knowing it couldn't stay. Knowing I couldn't last.

There is a clearly understood but rarely spoken ascension plan for recent arrivals to New York City, but you can only see it through if you stick around. We see the plan play out in bizarre real-time flashbacks as Carrie meets up with her girlfriends

Charlotte, Miranda and Samantha in the opening scene of *Sex and The City 2*. After more than a decade of watching these woman date, drink, brunch and bitch, in that single scene we finally saw where they all came from: Carrie met Charlotte late at night on the subway. She served Miranda during her stint as a salesgirl at Bloomingdale's, and first encountered Samantha when she was bartending at CBGB (because of course she was). Now they are powerful, well dressed, and so rich they take the very existence of public transport as a personal insult. The levels of career and physical and emotional success they achieve in the city are not possible anywhere else, and we're supposed to look at their lives and feel inspired; we should aspire to replicate them. Young female writers, especially, should want to *be* Carrie, who funded her high-heeled, martini-soaked lifestyle by writing one stream-of-consciousness column each week.

Before I arrived, I knew this glossy ideal was more murky and smudged in reality – I wasn't *that* naive. I'd seen *Broad City* when it was a YouTube webseries about two girls avoiding people they don't like on the subway, lugging all their possessions in huge tote bags to an intimidatingly fancy brunch situation, and sweating in a cramped bodega where creeps are lurking around every corner. That was the image of the city I expected, and it was the one I got. I kept a detailed diary during the first weeks of my trip, and at some point during the fourteen-hour flight, I wrote: 'I'm already feeling a little homesick. I'm glad I'm doing this; it's exciting! It's New York City! I guess I'm just pensive.' My instinct was tellingly a far cry from the excitement the city should have been conjuring up.

After my first day at work, I headed home to Williamsburg to eat dinner and watch Netflix. That morning, my boss had taken all the inhabitants of the company's New York office – him, me, and another Australian girl – for coffee at the nearby Ace Hotel, where he laid out our new game plan. That plan effectively was: each of us is in charge of a different part of the company, dig? I was doing the same job I'd been doing for two years already, only more intensely. Plus, without the reliable flock of interns who'd helped me in Melbourne, I was doing it alone until I could build up an American team. The day was exhausting and by the time I made it home, I needed to reboot. I was too self-conscious to eat out alone, and too accustomed to Melbourne's pre-food delivery app boom to realise I could have dinner *brought to me*, so I set about trying to locate it. I didn't know where anything was in the kitchen of my sublet, and it took me forever to find anywhere nearby that sold hot meals. I ventured into a vegan bakery to order a sandwich, but they were closing up and only had stale brownies leftover from the day. I bought one, tossed it into my bag and kept walking. By the time I reached the supermarket, I was starving, tired and immediately out of my element. I had been terrible at gauging the value of fresh produce in Australia, where the metric system was familiar and ubiquitous – *Sure, eight dollars for a kilo of bananas sounds good. How much can a banana weigh? Like, nine grams?* – but here, surrounded by ounces and pounds, I was truly baffled. The holiday fun of my first weekend wore off immediately as tears pricked at my eyes and I realised, suddenly, belatedly: *This is my life now. I will go to work every day and try to survive at all other times.* I realised in an instant that I didn't know anything. The month I'd spend alone before Anton arrived suddenly seemed too long. I hadn't planned or researched enough in advance, and I was overwhelmed by the first of what would become daily confusions. I made it home, took deep breaths to stave off an imminent and inevitable panic attack, and grilled a piece of fish for dinner before going to bed. Being out of my depth would become the norm.

At the time I was 21 years old. In retrospect, I was a baby, and it's reasonable that I hesitated and wobbled when I tried to orient myself in a foreign city with a notorious reputation for challenging even the most seasoned residents. But back then, I was the oldest I'd ever been and I thought I could handle it; I mean, I'd moved two states away on my own when I was eighteen and that was difficult at first but turned out to be great! I had always been an overachiever, and always seemed to impress people without trying just by virtue of being younger than they assumed I was. I played coy, but really loved being praised. But here, in a new place all alone, I would have to work a lot harder to achieve even a base level of success, and even if I somehow managed it, there might not be anybody around to notice. I was performing for myself alone, and I had stage fright.

Everything I'd always been able to do easily became immediately more difficult, from feeding myself to remembering how to talk to the people I love. Every time I Skyped with somebody at home, I'd dread the moment they stopped updating me on their lives to ask for news from me. I grappled for fun or exciting stories to tell, omitting the reality: I was too broke to do much of anything and even if I had some money, I'd be too scared or lonely to. The pressure to just survive was so immense that it left no time to be thoughtful or create, or just be.

Once he arrived, Anton unintentionally taught me how to be a good roommate and friend – mostly because our closeness revealed, quickly, how badly I was performing in that role. I was

lonely in my life in New York and unfairly expected Anton to fill
the role of all the friendships I'd left behind. Without knowing
how to communicate how my sense of self was dissolving each
day I spent living there, or how displaced I'd started to feel
as he settled into life in the city with his new school friends
and a boyfriend, I resorted to passive-aggressive silences and
snark. Not to reduce all girl-and-gay-man best friendships to
the obvious comparison, but I was Grace, in season one of
Will and Grace, when she leaves her boyfriend and moves in
with Will, then feels put out that he doesn't immediately centre
his life around hers. I thought, at 21 with a year of part-time
professional work and three sharehouses in my life experience
arsenal, I was ready for anything. Reading that sentence now,
I can see clearly how totally fucking blind I was going into
it all. Now, with the benefit of hindsight, I can tell you with
certainty that the only thing worse for a friendship than when
two people can't communicate, is when they can't communicate
and live together in a tiny apartment with two rooms – one of
which contains a bed that they share every night because they're
too broke to get a two-bedroom. Anton was my one link to my
old life, the one where I was stable and secure and okay, and
eventually I felt distance being planted between us, one that I
only helped widen.

Anton and I had met at university and become attached at
the hip soon after. We made internet comedy videos together
and laughed at the idea of becoming like Romy and Michele
watching *Pretty Woman* from our twin beds in the room we'd
share when we arrived in New York together. The reality wasn't
that far off; we made believe as a couple to get temporary sublets
across the city, because two-bedroom apartments were outside

our price range and because our total lack of credit history and social security made it impossible to get a lease.

I researched neighbourhoods, scoured sublet newsletters and scheduled apartment viewings. Once we arrived at each new place, Anton charmed the landlords while I did silent mental maths to calculate if we could afford the security deposit and how long it would take us to get to work and school every day. We moved at least eight times across Brooklyn and Queens that year, living everywhere from Fort Greene and Astoria to Bushwick (a few times) and Greenpoint. Each time a rental came to an end – after periods as short as five days and as long as four months – we re-packed our suitcases, hauled our books in tote bags and performed complicated relocation choreography.

We'd take turns propping open doors to load everything from our old place into waiting town cars, and do it in reverse when we arrived somewhere new. It was an exhausting project, but one we started to get really good at. My favourite day during that whole year was when we loaded in to an apartment in Fort Greene where we'd be staying for just two weeks. The beautiful brownstone had a projector screen, a Sodastream and a sweet cat named Widget that Anton and I still, years later, get emotional about leaving behind. After we unpacked, I ordered us food that we ate on the couch while watching *Sex and the City* all afternoon. With each temporary transplantation and our growing inability to discuss the ever-widening wedge between us – both emotionally and, at night when we went to bed, literally – our relationship slowly became more fractured. But on those moving days it felt like we were a real team.

Work didn't get easier, but I slowly became better at it. Running the website alone relied on being aware of new films and bands and labels that would make good stories, and New York gave me access to the people making the work I'd inevitably write about. One week I would be flying to Austin to cover twenty films in four days from the South by Southwest film program, another I might be downing free whiskey at a MoMA members' night and re-enacting a scene from *Manhattan* with an equally soused Anton.

I loved fashion but had always been too sweaty and scrappy and chubby to be accepted as someone who knew anything about it. Fashion weeks in New York felt at once like a place where I could both really understand the art, and never really get the measure of it. I'd arrive in the office early in the morning during those seasons, before hustling to the subway to make it to a show in time to stake out a spot on the riser at the end of a runway, my tiny SLR camera dwarfed by those of the Reuters and Style.com photographers, whose long lenses slid past my face, clicking threateningly. I'd take pictures and capture video, then avoid visiting celebrities as I snaked backstage to ask designers and stylists a few questions, before high-tailing it back to work to process it all and get a story up on the site.

I relished in acting ambivalent about the whole thing; I sat cross-legged in a gutter outside the backstage entrance to a show I was due to cover, eating a hot dog and hoping my presence made life a little bit hard for the street style photographers who skulked around like vultures snapping photos of models waiting for their turn to be made-up in the designer's vision. For all the fakery and posing, I loved seeing the way the industry operated.

One day I got to visit the studio of Eleven Objects, my favourite accessories label, as they put the finishing touches on their first collection of apparel inspired by both Peter Saville's album artwork for New Order, and Mozart. I felt swollen with pride the next week when I saw models wearing those pieces at a presentation in a gallery space, filled with the sound of a string quartet covering New Order songs. Another day I profiled the designer of a tiny label in Brooklyn on the last day she could have her pieces produced before her machinists closed up shop for Chinese New Year. We talked about Dan Flavin, Anton's favourite artist whose work he'd introduced me to on my first visit to the MoMA, and I helped her load her finished pieces into a cab as we left her tiny studio. Coldness and exclusion run through the veins of the fashion world, but there is nonetheless a heart pumping in the centre of it. The humanity I encountered beneath the glamour and assigned seating cancelled out any of the stress, weirdness or sidelong looks I got from a photographer when he complimented my sandals, before learning they were from Urban Outfitters. He turned up his nose almost immediately.

I never studied how to be an editor or writer (HI THANKS FOR READING MY BOOK CAN U TELL?), so that year of work was the deep end I almost drowned in, then finally figured out how to dog-paddle through. I might not have had everything figured out; I might've been a few years away from knowing what a semicolon *really* did, but I worked out how to be a boss whom people would like working with and for. One night I schlepped down Houston Street through the steaming hot spring rain to Mercury Lounge. I was there to interview Jeremy and Elizabeth from the UK band Summer Camp, whose outsider view of America informed their teen movie-themed songs and correlated with my own references for the country. We talked for ages about John Hughes, *Sassy* magazine and

My So-Called Life, and I struggled to keep my composure as the serious and objective editor writing a proper profile when I just *liked* someone so obviously and openly. During their show, they performed songs I loved in front of clips from the movies we'd bonded over, but at some point my joy was replaced with confused cynicism.

Since arriving in New York, I'd encountered so many people who only saw value in or use for the people they could aggressively network, and I never quite made the grade. I subconsciously entered so many situations assuming I'd be read as useless, but of course a band would want to be friendly and sweet if it meant I'd write positive things about them. During that Summer Camp gig I wondered if I had been sucked in by people successfully schmoozing the reporter. I pushed the notion out of my head the moment Elizabeth stepped off the stage during the song 'Losing My Mind'. She wandered through the crowd, singing delicately at the infatuated audience members. When she reached me, she lay her head on my shoulder and sang the final words of the song – and the show – directly to me. Some people are just good.

That doubt was the poison that New York seemed to pump into my mind like tear gas. I couldn't relax. I was on edge always: about money or men or my job or debt or my relationship with Anton, which was struggling under the weight of my unhappiness and our intimate living situation. I retreated into myself; instead of treating New York like a holiday, it became the great expectation I could never hope to live up to.

Everything is heightened when it happens in those five boroughs, the bad and the good. I had dipped into depressive episodes before in my life but had nothing with which to compare the full-body dread, exhaustion and hopelessness that swept over me that year. Hauling myself out of bed in my and Anton's Astoria apartment every morning during winter was overwhelming, to say the least. Every day before work, I was crying before I even opened my eyes. Deciding to finally pick up and read his copy of *The Bell Jar* on my morning commutes to work during that time was either the best or worst decision I've ever made, but it at least brought me to an inarguable conclusion: the biggest, brightest city in the world had turned me into the smallest, dullest version of myself. Like Esther Greenwood, I didn't know what I was doing in New York. I had become like that woman on the internet who takes her huge pet python to the vet to find out why it hasn't been eating and has been sleeping with her every night. Like that snake, the city was studying my weaknesses as it prepared to eat me alive.

How could I complain, though, when I'd never even had a passport before I flew to live there, and all of a sudden I could see the top of the Empire State Building from my office window? How could I complain when the best falafel and shawarma in the city was served from a truck at one end of my street, and at the other end was a McDonald's that, for no reason at all, served the neon green St Patrick's Day milkshakes year-round? How could I complain about being *so* broke that I shared a bed platonically with my best friend in our fourth-floor walk-up in Queens above a Greek cake shop owned by a suspicious landlord, when that description alone sounded romantic, just by virtue of it being a story that could only happen in New York? (And also when the stairs on that walk-up smelled like vanilla cupcakes all day every day?) That stuff sounds really cool, and if it happened on a short holiday or to a friend or in a movie I'd probably be totally charmed by those situations and that city. I'd likely associate life in the city to those huge IKEA canvases of inky black and white streetscapes with neon yellow cabs streaking by. But the daily reality of living in a place that tries its hardest to challenge and intimidate and overwhelm you every day is the part edited out of *Sex and the City*, the part that creeps into the edges of *Broad City* and makes cameo appearances in *Girls* and *Frances Ha* and other movies or shows about white ladies in New York.

One day, while masquerading in the role of the Professional Young Editor at a meeting in the lobby of the Ace Hotel, I looked past my coffee date's head and saw Susan Sarandon step through the doors of the hotel. She paused for just a second, before striding past the banks of people on laptops and into the Opening Ceremony store nearby. Suddenly, I couldn't concentrate on my conversation or the coffee in front of me because my mouth was filled with the taste of the generic brand candy-coated chocolates I'd spent my pocket money on when I was six, the ones I shovelled into my mouth in tiny fistfuls as I stared, transfixed, at Susan playing Janet, dancing in her bright white underwear in *The Rocky Horror Picture Show*. I might've been in the middle of New York City, but I could feel my family around me when I saw Janet in that moment, and it made me feel at home so suddenly and severely. I dropped the mask and ended the meeting for the honest, unprofessional reason: 'I'm sorry, I need to meet Susan Sarandon.'

That day, I broke the number-one rule of encountering a celebrity in the wild: I reacted. I didn't play it cool and act like this was an everyday occurrence. I paid for the coffees, walked terrifyingly quickly into Opening Ceremony and proceeded to pretend to shop for patterned socks while desperately scoping out the store. Susan was gone, but I felt bizarrely assured in a way I hadn't in months. I was suffocated by an overwhelming sense of home in a place that couldn't be farther from it.

When Facebook serves me up memories from June and July that year, they start out so excited. *I got my visa! I changed all my colourful plastic money to green paper money! I'm seeing all my friends for the last time in god knows how long!* As the months go on, the tone of my updates shifts, and I can retroactively see myself withdrawing. The masquerade of 'Here's a photo of Al Franken on the street!' was covering up the extreme ineptitude I felt every day at my job, and the unavoidable feeling of *doing* New York wrong every day.

No matter how hard I tried, how much money I spent, or how infrequently I spoke to my friends and family at home for fear that one more conversation would be the straw that broke the homesickness camel's back, I couldn't make New York work for me. I didn't exist there, as a Hasidic man named Hershey, from whom I was trying to rent an apartment in deep, outer Brooklyn, told me soon after I arrived.

In line at my first UCB show, I'd met a friend of a friend who had told me of the time she went to shake a Hasid's hand after a business meeting, and felt as though she had offended him. Knowing that Hershey was a traditionally observant Jew and hoping to impress him enough to score his dope two-bedroom, I made polite conversation when we met during the apartment inspection, but I didn't make any moves to shake his hand. I felt like I'd avoided a potential faux pas and succeeded in at least one job I'd taken up in the city.

I was open with Hershey about the fact that I'd just moved to New York City from Australia, and about my total absence of rental history in America. 'It's okay,' he told me, 'call me tomorrow and we'll discuss details.'

I felt hopeful for the first time since I'd arrived, and the next day, after telling Anton all about the apartment I'd found us that would mean we'd no longer have to share a bed or move every other month, I stepped onto the damp green street of the Flower District outside my office and dialled Hershey's number. 'You're the Australian,' he said when I introduced myself. It wasn't really a question, but I said yes anyway.

'We met yesterday and I'm just calling to confirm my interest in the apartment.'

'You have no credit, no social,' he told me, repeating the issues I'd raised with him, before he'd assured me it would work out regardless.

'That's right,' I said, eager to hear his solution.

'You do not exist in this country,' he said, before hanging up. I was shocked and upset and dreaded telling Anton, but I knew Hershey was right: New York didn't know I existed and even if it did, it wouldn't care if I left.

I am not the only one. I was not the first and I will not be the last. And that's an idea New York drills into you: you are not special. You are one of many thousands who dog-paddle through the days, exhausting yourself with the mere effort of keeping your snout above water, grasping onto and saving any small victories that float by. 'The city had beat the pants off me,' John Steinbeck wrote in 1953, for the *New York Times*, in a piece called 'Making of a New Yorker' that echoed the exhausting experience I'd mimic half a century later. He came to the city in the 1920s to work gruelling eighteen-hour days on the construction team that built Madison Square Garden. He quit after seeing a man fall to his death from the scaffolding, and returned to California in 1926. (He'd later betray us deserters and move back east, where he lived until his death.) 'Whatever it required to get ahead, I didn't have it,' he wrote. 'I didn't leave the city in disgust – I left it with the respect plain, unadulterated fear gives.' Admitting this absence of ability – especially for something as basic as simply surviving – is demoralising but eventually becomes essential if you have any hope of moving on from it.

I avoided facing the fear for months, but as my relationship with Anton deteriorated further every day, I knew I had to give it up. I asked him to have dinner with me one night in February, after he finished class at NYU. It was the first time we'd spent together in weeks; he'd stay late at school during the week, coming home after I was asleep like an avoidant husband in a movie, and spend the weekends at his boyfriend's house. I'd spend those lonely times vacillating between resenting him for leaving me and kicking myself for behaving in ways that made me impossible to be around. We sat in an awkward middle-ground between silence and small talk, before I pointed out that I hadn't been myself lately. Or, at least I tried to say that before I started crying immediately. Every difficult conversation I'd avoided the last few months swam in the tears that fell into my fries. He asked if I wanted to move back home, and I was equal parts devastated that he'd said it and relieved that I didn't have to be the one who did. I was finally confronting how hard it had been, how acutely I'd been feeling everything in my bones. We talked about the logistics of leaving, and Anton reassured me it would not be a failure on my part. I tried to accept that, but had trouble; I'd been terrified of failing my whole life, hated doing anything wrong, and here I was, unable to just *live in a place*.

After months of vaguely moody posts about loneliness and glum days on Instagram, I couldn't hide the packing boxes and suitcases that had begun to accumulate in the background of my life and photos. When I finally announced to my handful of friends and followers on social media that I was leaving, the response was an instant reminder of that invisible, contagious effect New York City has. Everyone was sad I was leaving, sad they couldn't 'live vicariously' through my photos anymore. Even when all I was doing was eating burgers and going to a gallery, the city and its ghost did all the work of romanticising the mundanity of those things to people outside of it.

That night over dinner marked an essential turning point in my and Anton's relationship, and we worked on mending the fracture that had threatened to split us in two for the last few months. The phrase 'clearing the air' is a well-worn cliché, but after doing it, we learned to inhale together again. We downed petrol-strength gin cocktails and performed ridiculous dances together at Fashion Week parties, returned to our favourite local taco spot for long dinners and plotted a comeback episode of the webseries we'd worked on together back in Melbourne. Soon the fact that I was leaving made me sad for the wasted time we'd missed in those dark months, and reassured me that I was leaving an even stronger relationship behind, one that we've been able to pick up seamlessly in the years since.

By the time I'd packed up to leave for good, it was April; the weather had changed and the city really put on a show.

For the first time it felt like it was turning on the charm for me. But, like a sweet boy who smiles and tells you nice things before ignoring your texts, I knew it wasn't going to last. The city was being a tease, but I was finally able to enjoy it in a way that I hadn't since I'd first arrived. Only this time, I had a handle on things: I could deal with an emotional day at work and a late train and a shady guy on the street when I knew there was a finite number of days still to come. Instead of taking events and museums and sunny afternoons and having Anton by my side for granted, I took advantage of them. I saw the city like a tourist for the first time since my first days there, and finally understood the appeal.

'I spent the worst year of my life in New York,' Ann Friedman once wrote in an essay. 'When I decamped for the West Coast ... I didn't feel failure or regret but relief. For me, New York is that guy I went out with only briefly and then successfully transitioned into friendship. We were always meant to be platonic.' Ann's closure with the city was essential assurance when I left, and she and I have more in common than just comparing New York to an unfulfilling relationship with a dude. It's taken a few years, but I can also see now that I didn't fail New York because I was too young or too broke or too depressed or too naive, nor because it was too hard or too harsh or too expensive. All of those things were true, but I didn't fail. I tried the city on, decided it didn't suit me, and went with a more flattering option.

I *was* embarrassed to leave though, embarrassed that I couldn't live up to the expectations of Frank Sinatra and Jay Z and *make it*, embarrassed that I never reached 'despising the subway' levels of *Sex and the City* success. 'Making it' there seemed like such a measure of success, one that proved your ultimate worth. For that reason, the failure in not coming out on top in New York was so much worse than if it had happened anywhere else.

Before I'd left Melbourne, my friend Greta had given me a card in which she'd written, 'No one will judge you if you want to come home.' When I first read it, at my going-away party, it was nothing but a sweet thought, a reassurance from a friend for a hypothetical situation that would never become my reality – *lol why would I ever want to come back here when I could be there?* Less than a year later, those same words gave me immeasurable comfort when I fretted over how much potential I might be wasting by not being able to see it through.

I've been back to the city twice, both visits lasting no longer than a fortnight. And in a way, I'm glad I dove in headfirst and tried living there before just taking a holiday, because it meant the possibility and glow doesn't affect me like I know it would have otherwise. I never leave New York dreaming of one day making it my home, because I know that the boozy midday breakfasts and long, meandering museum visits would never be norm. You can't afford to load up on Dean & DeLuca grain salads and Russ & Daughters lox and bagels to eat leisurely in the park when you have rent to deal with. The holiday image of New York is so temporary but such a persuasive drawcard, and I know myself well enough now to know I'd fall victim to it if I didn't have the memory of what its reality is behind the glow. I'm glad to be immune to the pull now. I don't romanticise that big, dirty, magical island in the way I did when it was nothing more than a faraway place I saw in movies and TV shows – not now that I've experienced the reality of living in an apartment so tiny you need to poo with the bathroom door open because it wasn't built to accommodate a toilet *and* a person.

After living in New York, most people are in need of a safe space to bounce back, or restore from their scratch disk. That decision I made right before I turned 22 wasn't just about leaving a job I'd outgrown. It wasn't just about moving closer to the people who write in cards the things I'd literally have to die to hear otherwise, and it wasn't just about trading New York in for anywhere else. It was about coming back to Melbourne and to myself, two things I realised had been left behind, along with my lost suitcase.

Steinbeck wrote that, for all of New York's ugliness and hard-won daily battles, 'there is one thing about it – once you have lived in New York and it has become your home, no place else is good enough.' No offence Johnny, but you're straight-up wrong. Downgrading from that legendary city to Melbourne sounds on paper like a step down, but in reality no other decision has made me feel as secure, confident and loved as that one did.

Melbourne has been a place that embraced me and allowed me to survive even when it was challenging. It is a place that gives people chances. I remember once hearing someone say that, here, you don't need to sell a bunch of records for people to come to your gigs, you don't need to be a huge name to have an art opening or book launch or any other creative endeavour. The city and the people in it will give you a chance to prove yourself. And if you fall on your butt and need to start from scratch, reinventing yourself with new passions or pursuits, they'll likely do the same thing the next time. You can make it here like you can't make it anywhere else, and you never get shut out for trying. Melbourne isn't an omnipresent barrier, forcing you two steps back for each inch of progress you make. It's literally won awards for being liveable, but it's also a city that helped me to survive.

After moving back, I made new friends and reconnected with old ones. I started my dream project that led to a great job and a writing career and this book. Not living in New York didn't limit my ambition at all; if anything, it made it more possible to write and think. One of the biggest articles I had published on an American website was written in my bedroom in Melbourne and subsequently shared on the *New York Times* app. I worked tirelessly to pay off the debts a year in New York left me with, and planned return trips to see Anton once I was in the black. Lying beside him on the grass after a picnic in Central Park, choking down a massive Dallas BBQ margarita, serenading him with Sheryl Crow songs at the Cobra Club karaoke night, and dancing to Carly Rae Jepsen in the sweaty Terminal 5 crowd with him on a cold night is undeniably better now that we're both living where we should be, even if it means we're not waking up in the same time zone anymore.

Ann Friedman said that she has to explain to diehard New York fans that escaping the city felt like she learned to breathe again. My return to Melbourne did more than just that – it proved Hershey wrong and reminded me that I exist.

CHAPTER 8

FAITHFUL

Despite having a sliver of what I truly think are psychic powers like Phoebe's in the first few episodes of *Charmed*, I am not a spiritual person. I believe a lot of what Jackie, the professional psychic, says in her readings on *Real Housewives of Melbourne*, but I am ultimately more cynical than I am hopeful. I think ghosts exist even if I never saw the one that apparently lives in a supposedly haunted hotel I once stayed in, but I don't really think that crystals or charms or wishes do much of anything. I'm baffled by astrology; learning that my behaviour and mannerisms were supposedly astrologically predetermined – and are mirrored in any other person born around the same time as I was – is difficult enough to comprehend on its own and, growing up, I resented the idea that I shared commonalities with people like Phil Collins, Shakira and Dr Dre, simply because we share a star sign. Over brunch at the Chateau Marmont (hahahaha I know, fuck this bitch, right?) during a holiday in LA, my friend Dylan explained that being born under Aquarius wasn't where my horoscope ended, that I also had to factor in rising signs and natal charts and other things I don't come close to understanding but terrify me nonetheless. It was too much to grasp so I just ate my $25 BLT in confusion and made a note to google it later.

Before I came to understand the things I thought and believed (or lack thereof), I desperately wanted to be religious. My mum grew up going to Sunday School and being taught by nuns who clapped her over the palm or made her stand up in class with her arms raised over her head as punishment. She was raised by my grandmother who was, and still is, anti-religion. Nonetheless, Mum reminded me when I asked, that I could practise whatever religion I wanted to. My childhood was the inverse of what kids raised in strict religious households experienced; they all seemed desperate to break away, but I wanted to know what it felt like to join in.

In primary school, it was accepted for even public schools like mine to inject religious education (or RE) into our classrooms. Once a week, someone from the community – never a pastor or priest or nun, always just a random Christian person – would spend an hour with us, teaching us about Jesus and Moses and all those other bros, with the aid of colouring books, songs and activities. Before the classes began, one or two kids were always excused and sent to the library. In the early years of school, it was the lone kid whose Muslim family ran the Turkish kebab shop in town; as I got older, it was the girls with box-dyed black hair and an expanding line-up of studs running the length of their ear. They were the people whose parents had ticked a box on a form asking that they be excused from RE, which now seems like something I'd want for myself or my hypothetical kids, but back then they always seemed like the odd ones out. They sat in the library while we traded Disciples Trading Cards handmade by the weird guy who yelled about the inevitable apocalypse on street corners and scribbled prophecies in Sharpie on his polo shirt. They had to read dumb books while we got to sing Bible verses set to pop melodies. (It was this practice that makes me, to this day, still mentally and melodically connect the passage from John 3:16 to the song 'Break My Stride' by Unique II.)

I never questioned the fact that 'religious education' meant 'Christian education'; nobody was teaching us about Judaism or Hinduism or Islam, despite the fact that families of people in our school practised those at home. I always assumed that stories about Jesus were what everybody learned and believed. Christian was the default, and from the outside, it seemed cool and attainable. The kids at my school who went to church and camps and youth groups had full calendars and tonnes of friends, all of whom shared an unspoken bond – some even went to other schools. (Which, as everybody knows, is the universal sign of enigmatic and interesting. Having friends at other schools is as worldly as you can hope to get in a small town.)

Despite her own agnosticism, Mum dutifully drove me to my friend Chrissy's church youth group one Thursday night. Chrissy was a regular there, and introduced me to other kids who eyed me suspiciously as we sat in the rumpus room of a suburban home, eating snacks. Eventually, someone turned on the TV and we watched a cool new movie called *Left Behind*. Starring Kirk Cameron, the movie showed a vision of the rapture, a moment in time when all true Christians are plucked from

their cars or homes or schools or – in one troubling scene – aero-
plane seats, and sent to heaven. Those left behind are punished
for their doubt or apathy with seven years of suffering. The
movie presented a horrifying version of events that seemed at
odds with what I thought Christianity was about; it (and the
people I watched it with) seemed to delight in the terror of
tribulation. Of the two options the movie gave me – to have
faith and be taken to heaven, or be a sinner who'd be smited,
or trapped in a pile-up when drivers are lifted from their cars
and into heaven – the obvious choice felt clear. I was grappling
with enough confusing images of God already – the concept of
something/someone/*anything* watching me when I was sleeping
or showering or on my knees was more unsettling than it was
comforting – but maybe I was just too new to it to see what
everyone else did. Maybe I had to try harder.

I went to church with Chrissy a few times after that, and
started getting the hang of youth group. Sometimes it was held
at the church and they served oven-baked chicken nuggets for
dinner. The other kids started picking me for their team when
we played games outside, and I relished in the laughs I got
when I whispered jokes about the Easter bunny during a movie
about Jesus's resurrection. When it came time to sign up for
the annual camp, I had my mum fill out the permission form.

That winter, I headed off to the camp in a nearby beachside
town where I'd be staying in a cabin with Chrissy, two of her
cousins and a group of girls I'd never met. All of them had
brought their personal Bibles; Cool Teen™ versions of the book
with illustrations and contemporary translations. The books
were all bound in colourful covers that held their pens and
notebooks, like saintly Lisa Frank Trapper Keepers. I didn't

even own a regular Bible, let alone a dope one like these, and didn't realise I would need one to fit in.

Along with classrooms and activity spaces, the camp had huge trampolines, a cafeteria with long, communal tables and a general store. There was one allocated day when we were all allowed to visit the store and buy lollies, chips, chocolates and soft drink. Jessie, a girl who slept on the bunk above mine, bought a fistful of paper sherbet packets, the kind that come with a tiny plastic trowel to shovel the powder easily into your mouth. That night in the cabin, while everyone else read Bible passages together, I listened in intently, trying not to be distracted by the white dust showering down on my face and neck from the top bunk. All of a sudden, Jessie started coughing. She kept going, until I realised she was choking on the fucking sherbet. Our cabin leader helped her to sit up, and sent me to take Jessie to first aid, where she invented an elaborate story about having asthma and forgetting to take her inhaler to bed with her. I was shocked that, after a week spent listening to bearded camp counsellors talking about honesty and forgiveness and trust that she could lie so blatantly and confidently. I left that camp having learned a lot of very basic rules for my new aspirational Christianity (the main one was effectively 'have a pray about it, that fixes anything!') but also realising that even cool teen Christians are full of shit sometimes.

At home, my parents were fighting a lot. I was old enough to understand how bad it was, but too young to see them as humans with their own brains and hearts and hopes beyond what my sisters and I needed on a daily basis. From the time I was nine, when we moved back to Bundaberg from Gympie, to when I was twelve and Dad told my sisters and I that he was moving out, Mum and Dad fought loudly and often. Almost every night I went to sleep to the sounds of them arguing, but it was only after coming home from camp that I tried to do something about it. I made an effort only because I needed something so badly and couldn't think of any other action to take, and I had finally been given the tools to make a change. I channelled what I'd learned at camp, and prayed. I did what I had been told, and prayed for what I wanted so that Jesus could make it happen. I didn't have a Bible and I wasn't christened but I did know what I wanted: for my parents to get a divorce so we could all stand a chance of being happy and getting a good night's sleep.

Every night of my life until that point, my mother had sung me to sleep. At my request, she'd sit on the edge of my single bed and sing pitchy versions of 'Edelweiss' from *The Sound of Music* and 'Morningtown Ride' by the Seekers, all while stroking my hair and shh-ing me. I remember it so vividly because she kept doing it until I was old enough to be too old to be sung to sleep. That's what I decided, anyway. My rationale for asking her to stop was that my sisters hadn't needed her to sing them to sleep when they were eleven. I replaced that ritual – of being soothed to sleep by my mum's voice and stroking palm – with my new prayers.

When we bump into unfair or uncomfortable experiences, we try to cobble together some semblance of a coping mechanism so we can make it out the other side. Logic often fails us, though, like when Anjelica Huston's character in the movie *50/50* learns her son has cancer and her instinct is to make him green tea, because she heard it reduces your risk of cancer by fifteen per cent. I could sense the rope that bound my parents together was starting to fray, and begged my new friend Jesus to just make it snap already, to get it all over with. When they told us, a year later, that my dad would be moving out, it felt like proof that prayers worked.

During the press tour for her 2011 film *Higher Ground*, Vera Farmiga said the story of Corinne, a woman whose born-again husband, Ethan, becomes heavily involved with an insular Christian sect while she struggles to find a way in, was motivated by what she saw as a universally human quest for salvation and desire to reach transcendence. Corinne's story is so familiar: she wasn't born into religion, but chose it for herself. When she and Ethan were just teenagers, they got pregnant and got married. While their baby, Abbey, slept in a beer cooler in the back of Ethan's band's van, he got distracted and drove the car off the road and into a lake. The band was safe, their gear was ruined and inside the floating cooler they found baby Abbey, safe and sound. 'God saved her, Corinne,' Ethan pointedly told his wife later, all logic abandoned in favour of hope. 'God saved us.' Corinne and Ethan grew up and found a chosen family in the church, one that resented her questions and desire to clarify the doubts that sprang up. She was told to listen and accept, not to speak.

Religion became something I picked up and put down when I needed it, or didn't. In the years connecting primary and high school I became friends with Laura, who was from an intensely Christian family. Her parents were staples in their local church and religion seemed to play a role in all the decisions she made and words she said. Once when we were arguing over a class project together, I offhandedly told her to shut up, and her hackles raised. She demanded to know how I could say words that Jesus hated. (Look, I haven't read the book cover to cover like Dave Rygalski did in *Gilmore Girls* so he could take the Bible-bashing Mrs Kim's daughter, Lane, to the prom, but I'm pretty certain Jesus never said, 'thou doth mustn't tell anyone to shut up'.) In the later years of high school, when Laura and I had well and truly drifted apart, the gossip mill spun wildly with the rumour that she'd unofficially, symbolically 'married' her boyfriend in the front yard of her parents' house to get around the whole 'celibacy until marriage' bit.

One Saturday night, years before any pretend weddings, I had a sleepover at Laura's house. We watched a movie on the couch, and her dad stood behind us the entire time, monitoring us and everything we were watching on TV. The next morning, over breakfast, I watched as his wife prepared him eggs and his son brought him juice. The eggs weren't cooked the way he wanted so he called out directions for how he liked them. All three members of his family jumped from their seats, each one desperately wanting to be the one to please him. Once he got his eggs, they took their seats, linked hands and prayed for one another. I'd known, theoretically, that religion could be designed around the needs of the man, the leader of the house, but never saw it play out in real life before then.

My dad cooked for us sometimes and did his own laundry. My grandpa tidied the house and made tea and patiently braided my and my sisters' hair, just as he'd done for his four daughters. In the grand scheme of Religious People Using Their Faith to Control Other People, raising a family to wait hand and foot on their patriarch is nowhere near the worst thing that can happen. It isn't even a blip on the radar of massacres and manipulation that the world endures because of deranged or influential devout people. We weren't an actively feminist or progressive family, but even as a kid I knew something was inherently backwards and outdated about this family who gave ten per cent of their income every Sunday to people who taught them to be subservient to the lazy man at the dining table.

After breakfast, I joined Laura's family at church. We sat together in a row of plastic seats arranged in a draughty hall. I didn't know the words to the songs everyone else knew without looking at sheet music. After the service, we were called up for Eucharist. When we all stood up to accept their wine and bread, Laura's mother stopped me, saying I needed to sit back down. She'd remembered a conversation we'd had months earlier in which I told her that, in my family, only my eldest sister had been christened. I hadn't, and because of that I wouldn't be allowed to share their snack of bread and grape juice. I'd spent the morning listening to everyone around me reminding me that I needed to be here, that I wasn't complete without the lessons I'd learn in that room. Now I discovered there was a criteria for belonging, and I didn't meet it. After that encounter, it was years before I'd step foot in a church again.

Throughout my early teens, the closest I came to religion was Mandy Moore movies. After introducing herself to the world as a sassy pop singer with a love of VW beetles in her breakout music video for 'Candy' (and later as a girl-next-door type with an enviable collection of Paul Frank pyjamas in one of the first teen magazines I ever bought with my own money), Mandy started acting in the early 2000s. She was in teen catnip *The Princess Diaries* (with my trio of boos: Anne Hathaway, Heather Matarazzo and Sofia Coppola's cousin from the band Rooney) and *How to Deal*, but sealed her spot in my pop culture lexicon forever after playing the pious cancer patient Jamie Sullivan in

A Walk to Remember and the Christian queen bee Hilary Faye in *Saved!* Both these characters had faith in lieu of personalities and used their religious credentials to lord themselves over their classmates.

In *A Walk to Remember*, Jamie passively pities her classmates who don't spend their weekends hangin' with the Lord, and warns bad boy Landon (played by Shane West) not to fall in love with her the moment they start spending time together. (Spoiler alert: he does and they end up getting married WHILE THEY ARE STILL IN HIGH SCHOOL . . . before she dies of leukaemia.)

Hilary Faye is a more evil and extreme incarnation of Jamie. She expects to be rewarded for her small sacrifices: she constantly reminds everyone what a good person she is for driving her wheelchair-bound brother, Roland, around in her van; she hosts a self-satisfied prayer circle in her home on behalf of her friend Mary's gay boyfriend in an attempt to 'save' him. At one point, Hilary Faye tries to abduct Mary and exorcise Satan from her. When Mary struggles free, Hilary Faye literally hurls a Bible at her, screaming, 'I am FILLED with Christ's love! You are just jealous of my success in the Lord.' After this sensationalised and ironic display, Mary has to remind her friend that the book is not a weapon.

Like cafeteria politics or corporate teams, religious social structures operate hierarchically, and what I saw in my life and in movies reinforced the idea that rising to the top required a superior sense of righteousness stemming from the power that believers can lord over those who aren't. As you ascend to the top of the fountain, by default, there will be people getting dripped on beneath you. A few years after extracting myself, I was pulled back into the whirlpool.

I spent the summer before Year 11 hanging out with three girls and a guy who all went to different schools. I knew them from parties and Myspace and hanging around our quiet town's shopping centres on Thursday nights when the shops were open late. We formed a close-knit bond and spent weekend nights crashing at one another's houses. My mum called them my 'bad influence friends' and tried, for the first and only time in my life, to ground me in an effort to prevent me from spending more time with them. It didn't work. We were inseparable.

It was with them, huddled inside a caravan parked under a house that had been raised on stilts, that I first smoked weed from a bong crafted out of a Coke can. My new friends taught me how to light the cone, when to inhale and how long to hold the smoke in my throat. The usual murky bong water I'd later come to recognise was replaced, in this instance, by a puddle of lukewarm Coke. It tasted sweet and nutty and delicious. On another night, someone's parents had gone out of town and we had the whole house to ourselves. Everyone else indulged in white powder that was either lowercase 'c' coke, or speed. (I couldn't tell the difference between them back then, and still couldn't now.) They got a little weed for me and I smoked it alone, totally defeating the social passing and giggling I thought was synonymous with smoking.

I'd never known a feeling of paranoia like I did after smoking weed that night. But I trusted these friends more than anything, more than it was probably safe to trust a band of teenagers with houses to themselves and such easy access to hard drugs. So when I sat outside on the verandah with my legs tucked up against my chest while one of them told me I was sitting in an invisible bubble, I believed her. I had faith in what she was telling me. From the outside, I'm sure I looked like a drama kid who'd never sipped a beer trying to act drunk; my words were melting together and my eyes were as wide as golf balls. I felt safe in that bubble and felt terrified when she told me that I'd die if it popped. I sat perfectly still, scared to breathe too deeply, holding frantic eye contact with my friend. She raised her finger and her eyes widened. 'You're in the bubble,' she reminded me, 'don't let it pop.' She brought her finger closer to my face and I begged her not to break the seal because I believed her words more than anything I'd ever believed before. I had so much faith in her and trusted her to keep me safe. She plunged her finger at my face. 'POP!' She laughed as I flinched and gasped for breath and fell over sideways, my knees still pressed against my chest.

Within a month, we were all back at school and, like the summer fling at the start of *Grease*, we knew we wouldn't see each other in the same way again. I turned sixteen, started my senior years of high school and as those relationships dissolved, I started to fall in with a new, diametrically opposed group.

It started like a sitcom or rom-com or some other kind of com. I was grocery shopping with my mum on a Saturday morning and my sister's friend, who worked at the supermarket, asked if we'd heard about the new guys who'd moved to town. They were three brothers, he said, and they're cute. Apparently their dad had moved to Bundaberg to run a new church and had brought his family with him; supposedly, the brothers were in a band; some girls in town had already added them as friends on Myspace *and they'd accepted*. If the girls and closeted gay boys in that town had run a newspaper, word of this arrival would've made the front page. Information was circulated throughout Bundaberg in the same hushed tones within a couple of days (which should be proof of how close our brains were to melting into a puddle and trickling out of our noses out of pure boredom).

It wasn't long before we'd meet and I'd learn that, for once, town gossip hadn't warped the reality of a situation. They were three brothers, two of them were high school age but none of them went to school. They were a Hanson-style family band, albeit one who only played at the youth-leaning church at which their dad was a pastor instead of in stadiums all over the world. It seemed that everyone in town had learned about the new arrivals, and even the most casual hangs with them would include a growing number of us, mostly girls, all in our late teens, trying to make an impression that would stick. One of those girls was Zoey. She and I became instantly close thanks to our love of the Molly Shannon movie *Superstar*, and I was able to be refreshingly honest with her about my real motivations for being there: I had a crush, as had been the case with Hanson after I first saw the 'Mmmbop' music video eight years earlier, on the youngest brother.

Zoey had been raised in a Christian household and, like Mary Katherine Gallagher in *Superstar*, was familiar with the processes of being a churchgoing person, while I wasn't really sure how to deal with the tithing, working bees and being nice to *everyone* (really? everyone? even if they suck?) that came along with it. But I was willing to pretend, to suck it up and work it out, if it meant I got to spend a few days a week with a cute boy I instantly decided I had a crush on without having had a real conversation with him.

In retrospect, if it hadn't involved such a conscious effort to warp who I inherently was as a person, being a regular church-goer was actually the perfect way to spend time with someone I liked; there were always events, trips to the movies or casual hangs happening during the week, and even if there weren't, I knew we'd see each other every Sunday morning. I relished the community it gave me; if I could show up to one place at the same time every weekend and know all my friends would be there, I'd still do it today. (It's the same reason why I love knowing *Game of Thrones* will be back for ten weeks every winter: it guarantees ten nights to spend eating pizza in a warm lounge room with my friends.)

The churchgoing life was so convenient and welcoming. Unlike the awkward high school parties where I desperately tried to fit in, no one ever questioned who invited me. After services, we'd go to someone's house to watch movies or spend hours bogarting the dining room of McDonald's. I made small talk with everyone and gave a few dollars. I sang the songs (even learned some of the words off by heart) and listened to the sermon afterwards. I felt like I was a part of a group, and got to spend time with cute, nice boys who wore skinny jeans even in summer. I tried really hard to absorb everything, all the while trying even harder to quiet the disbelief in my head.

I worked so hard to be a good little fake Christian. I was careful with my words, holding back on swearing and only laughing at the jokes my new friends co-signed. I read *Chicken Soup for the Teenage Soul* and went to see Christian rock bands in concert when they came to town, shifting uncomfortably from foot to foot as the concerts inevitably descended into sermons and audience members were called forward to be prayed for, or saved.

Going to church as a teenager felt like when I watched porn for the first time and knew I was supposed to be feeling something but I knew THIS wasn't it. Both times, I mimicked what I knew I was supposed to do, but was ultimately overwhelmed with how unconvincing it all was; the first time was because the video my friends had rented from Blockbuster didn't actually show any Ds or Vs, and the second time was because everyone seemed to buy that 'speaking in tongues' was a legit thing and not just nonsense words someone had clearly practised at home, ready to recite on Sunday morning. In *Higher Ground*, Corinne's closest friend in the church, Annika, starts speaking a foreign-sounding jumble of words one day while they're out on the lake. When Corinne asks what it is, Annika tells her it's a prayer language. Corinne is desperate to reach this supreme level of holy communication, and proceeds to practise forming her mouth around strange sounds and willing the Lord to visit her and speak through her. If spirituality doesn't come naturally, it comes by force.

During a lesson on theology at school, my beloved history teacher told us that, despite being an atheist, he had read the Bible, the Torah and the Qur'an. 'You've read the Bible?!' one of my classmates asked, shocked. He explained that he couldn't confidently disagree with the principles of a text without knowing it first. One of my other classmates, a god-fearing teen who aspired to be a missionary and spread the word to sinners the world over, had her hackles raised during that entire class, calling out what she saw as mistakes or inconsistencies. During a conversation about how our genetic make-up and geographic situation often dictates our faith (or lack thereof), she said she'd have found Jesus no matter where she was born. Our teacher asked if she thought she'd still be a Christian if she were born, say, in Pakistan, in the country with the second-largest Muslim population in the world. My classmates and I shook our heads in unsurprised disbelief when she insisted on her delusion that, yes, Jesus would have found her no matter what, instead of conceding to reality: that she happened to be born to a mother who would take her to church every Sunday and send her to camps like the one I'd gone to with Chrissy.

Churches run on blind conviction like hers. I couldn't verbalise the doubt I felt when I was still going to one every Sunday because I feared it would give me away as a fraud among the flock, and I'd lose the friends I so appreciated having. I didn't really buy what the church was selling, but a lot of people did, and they were people I wanted in my life, so what was the harm in faking it a little longer?

During the time I was a regular at the church, it started filling up with more and more people I knew from my BC (Before Church) life, including a couple of the people I'd been so close to the summer before, my 'bad influence friends'. The flow-on effect of cute boys moving to a town and lowkey converting adoring girls and their friends worked a treat. A badboi surfer at my school, to whom I'd been close since we were thirteen because of our mutual appreciation for nasal emo music, started coming along on Sundays. We shared a silent understanding that what happened there wouldn't be shared with anyone at school. One day, when I was walking from one classroom to another, we crossed paths and he pulled me aside. 'I was sitting outside last night looking at the stars,' he told me, 'and it was like . . . *God made all of that.*' He was so sure, and filled with so much hope that I couldn't say, 'Yeah, *apparently*. See you in science class!'

When he was preparing for his role as Corinne's husband Ethan in *Higher Ground*, actor Josh Leonard said he had to spend a significant amount of time researching how people just *believe* in things, logic be damned. I spent that year trying so hard to believe, wanting so badly to feel the comfort and assurance everyone else seemed to, but I just couldn't. I was filled with too much doubt and cynicism to really have faith in anything greater.

One night, while we were all silently praying with our heads bowed and our eyes closed, my friend, who had started playing the drums in the house band, started to fidget in his seat. His phone was ringing and it wasn't on silent. His customised ringtone echoed out into the room before he could switch it off. The song it played was REM's 'Losing My Religion'. I laughed, typed a note into my phone to write about it one day, and now, ten years later, I'm doing that, while realising this was the moment I stopped trying so hard.

In *After the Thrones*, hosts Andy Greenwald and Chris Ryan discussed the shifting beliefs of Tyrion Lannister in the season six finale of *Game of Thrones*. Before then, he'd been a judgemental cynic, but in that episode we saw him flip to being a willing follower, full of optimistic hope.

Born to a noble house – including a father who hates him and twin siblings more interested in acquiring power and fucking each other than caring for anyone else – Tyrion has spent his life surrounded by people declaring what and who to believe in, as though there is one right answer for everyone. A true cynic, he never took the bait. Until he met Daenerys Targaryen, the daughter of the king killed by Tyrion's brother. Her political manoeuvring, human compassion and supernatural abilities that enable her to birth dragons and walk through fire changed something within him. The more time he spent with her, the lower his guard dropped until he allowed himself to be open and vulnerable; until he could just follow her without needing to be begged or convinced. 'Family, gods, kings, myself: it was often tempting, until I saw where belief got people. So I said no thank you to belief. And yet, here I am. I believe in you,' he tells her, before they set sail to conquer another land. 'It's embarrassing, really.' In this moment, Tyrion exemplifies both the best-case scenario – having your devotion received by someone worthy of assigning it to – and the vulnerability required to surrender your better judgement.

'Cynics are always looking for something to believe in,' Ryan says of Tyrion (and, lowkey, all of us) on *After the Thrones*, before putting his finger on precisely why that's so difficult when belief is rooted in mysticism or invisible beings in the sky: 'I think that the reason they're cynical is because they can't find that person.'

I worked so hard to believe in a way that seemed to come easily to everyone else. I tried time and again – with Chrissy and Laura and now with these cute teenagers who found a way to work Gym Class Heroes songs into church services – but I always felt like I was waiting to be convinced instead of hoping to be enlightened. No matter how many times I attended church or how many conversations I had with Zoey in her car afterwards, I never stopped feeling like the new kid desperately trying for acceptance. Church began to feel like being at a convention for passive-aggressive experts; it was like being talked *about*, never to, as if God was someone I had a crush on who didn't know I exist (or, if he did, he was playing hard to get and negging me).

In the end, I stopped going to church after one more sermon I couldn't connect to or agree with. The pastor, my friends' dad, was talking at length about being a kind and good person. They were the central tenets of Christianity, he said, but you couldn't express them properly if you weren't a true believer. Sitting there in the uncomfortable plastic seat, I thought of my mum and my grandparents and my friends who had no interest in stepping foot inside a church, but who had been nothing but kind and good to me. I thought about the person I was a year earlier, and the person I would be if I stopped showing up every Sunday morning. I knew that person would be as good as anyone speaking in tongues in that room. *Fuck this,* I thought. I left shaking with rage that day, and never went back.

Within a couple of years, I'd moved away from Bundaberg and all the people in it. Zoey and I kept in touch, and when she visits we always end up talking about those years we spent in a strange zone where everyone was trying to impress with their piousness.

I'd soon find a family in the heavy smokers and drinkers and musicians who didn't need religion to tell them to be kind to me. I found a place where I was accepted, not interrogated, where I felt connected instead of competitive. I learned all the words to the songs they sang in the dark back rooms of pubs and bars where we came together on Sunday afternoons . . . and Thursday, Friday and Saturday nights. I learned what it meant to truly believe in the places where the soles of my shoes melded to the sticky carpet. Communion came in the form of cheap lukewarm beer and hastily rolled cigarettes, and this time I was allowed to take it. It was poured into my glass in living rooms with bad sound systems or band rooms with slightly better ones. We didn't wear symbols on chains around our necks, but had them stamped on our wrists with watery ink.

I have two posters on my wall that I found at an antique market. They were printed by the American Bible Society, and vaguely remind me of ones hanging in that rumpus room years ago where we watched *Left Behind*. Only, instead of warning me that I'll be left to burn if I don't believe, one reminds me that LOVE IS PATIENT, while the other tells me to REJOICE IN HOPE. On my wrists I have tattooed the pillars of my own type of faith. My right wrist says CONFIDENCE and my left one says KINDNESS. I don't need a book to tell me they are important to me. I know myself well enough now to know what I need and what I believe.

CHAPTER 9

HE LIED ABOUT DEATH

The story of my most complex formative relationship is one I've never told, but one you've probably heard before. In her 2014 memoir, Lena Dunham talked about falling in love with a boy over AIM, and the shock of learning he had 'died'; at the time of writing this, *Catfish: The TV Show* is going into its fifth season on MTV; and, a few years ago, Australian news headlines were frothing over the revelation that *Australian Idol* winner Casey Donovan once entered into a long and emotionally manipulative relationship with a woman masquerading as a man online.

Despite all of these contemporary references, my go-to touchstone for falling in love on the internet is still *You've Got Mail*. Discussions of online dating fill my mind with images of Tom Hanks warming up his fingers before punching out a transmission to 'Shopgirl' (Meg Ryan's character's screenname). Eight years after that film showed the world that the internet could be used for more than just pornography, I was unknowingly crafting my own online story with the first and, at the time of writing this, only person to ever tell me they loved me.

I've moved into more than a dozen houses and apartments and probably illegal sublets in the decade since I made a scrapbook of all my online conversations with Nate, but in all the packing and unpacking, I've never been able to bring myself to throw it away. Its cut-and-pasted contents include my handwritten but unsent love letters, printouts of private messages and public blog posts, and transcriptions of text messages I felt the need to preserve, all sent to or from someone who carved out a space in my life and my family's dial-up internet bill for two years.

'I know that I have spent hours crying over you,' I wrote – on what was then freshly tear-stained paper – when I was sixteen years old, 'I know that other boys who have made me cry were irrelevant. I know that you were worth every tear.' At the time I thought these earnest proclamations of love were the height of emotional maturity, but they were more likely just a roll-on effect of listening to nothing but Dashboard Confessional, The Used and Taking Back Sunday on loop from 2002 to 2007. This flimsy scrapbook is a very tangible, very permanent record of a relationship that was totally ephemeral and, thanks to the dissolution of Myspace and MSN, totally invisible now.

That was how he and I originally got to know each other; he added me on MSN one day, out of nowhere, and we'd occasionally IM about totally innocent things: music (he told me he was in a hardcore band and would send me songs I pretended to like); Chris Lilley shows; and our favourite snack foods. I was fifteen, as-yet-unkissed and perennially horny at the time. At school, the boys treated me like either a boner-killer or nothing more than a friend, but every day after schlepping home from the bus stop and waiting for the internet to dial up, Nate would be there to talk. He'd tell me about his girlfriends and never seemed to notice that my considered thoughts on *The Godfather* and Australian hardcore bands were eerily similar to what was on Wikipedia. He was nineteen and lived two states away, in the suburbs outside Melbourne. Despite thinking he was cute and that his tattoos and lip ring were cool, I didn't invest a whole lot of emotional energy into our conversations and had no idea we were in the early stages of what would (spoiler alert) become a drawn-out and dramatic catfish.

I know saying I was initially ambivalent sounds like some kind of retrospective self-preservation, because it's easy to say my heart wasn't in it when it's ten years later and hindsight has awarded me the gift of knowing better. But it's true. Maybe it was the years of boys in my small town going out of their way to tell me they weren't attracted to me, but there was nothing that told me to expect anything more than friendship from Nate. When we first connected, he purely offered me a place to feel cool and funny and likeable – something that meant everything considering the scarcity of people I'd met who could both relate to my interests and open my eyes to new ones. It wasn't until we took things offline, and starting texting and calling one another just as regularly as we'd IM, that 'likeable' started to become something more.

For months, I didn't know what was going on in the game he was playing. When he'd call me on a Saturday night while I was drinking sugary vodka pineapple concoctions in someone's backyard and ask me to stay on the phone for so long that I effectively missed the entire party, I didn't think anything of it. He made me laugh, and those phone calls took me outside the mundane high school drama that suffocated every party. When he said it'd be easier if I stayed home on a Saturday night so we could talk online or on the phone without being interrupted by my friends at a party or my sister needing to use the phone, I didn't think anything of it. It would be quieter if we talked when I was alone in my bedroom instead of around my friends. When he called me one morning in September 2006, I thought he wanted to hear about the life-changing night I'd just had at a Dashboard Confessional concert (no big deal but Chris Carrabba touched my hand and I walked out afterwards yelling, 'I could die now and be happy!' into the night air), but instead he told me he had been diagnosed with lung cancer and had just six months to live.

This would, of course, reveal itself to be the first, biggest and most unforgiveable lie he'd tell me, but at that point it was a secret that bound me to him. After that point, the phone calls and texts became more frequent and more familiar. He needed me now, in a way no one had before. A few weeks later I took my first ever plane trip to visit my friend Sarah, whom I'd met on Myspace (because it was 2006), in Melbourne. It felt like the perfect time for Nate and me to finally meet in person. We made plans to meet outside a skate shop in the city and I was nervous when the time came, but it was all for nought: he didn't turn up.

When Tom Hanks's character Joe Fox (screenname NY152) showed up to meet Shopgirl (holding a book with a rose in it, as they'd agreed over AOL), he had Dave Chappelle there to peer in the window first and tell him what Shopgirl looked like. Joe found out it was his IRL professional nemesis, Kathleen, and so he went inside to tease her about being 'stood up' by her date. All I got was a text from Nate a few hours later telling me he was sorry, that he'd been worried I'd be disappointed by him. He asked if we could meet again in a few days at Ringwood train station, in the outer Eastern suburbs of Melbourne. Confused and hesitant but not enough to keep me from spending time with a handsome older friend, Sarah and I rode trains for hours to get to Ringwood. Again, we were left standing in the rain, waiting for Nate, who wouldn't answer his phone and didn't show up. By this point I just figured my casual pal, who shared a fragment of my musical taste, was flakey and nervous, and thought no more of it.

That night, at Sarah's house, I got a private message on Myspace from Nate's account, only it wasn't him typing: it was someone who identified themselves as his best friend's girlfriend, there to tell me that Nate had been hospitalised and had been saying my name in his sleep. That's why he didn't show up, she said. A few days later, he told me via text message he was in love with me and, when I didn't say it back, he wrote, 'I guess it's hard to believe the words of a dying man.'

It's so fucked up, so transparently bullshit. But I bought it hook, line and sinker. (Does that make me a fish, even if *he* was the one doing the catfishing? This analogy is TBC.) Writing this now is perhaps one of the most embarrassing things I've ever done, because every single link in this chain of events sets off alarm bells and sounds like a chapter from *Manipulating Lonely Teens – For Dummies*. But it felt so real in the moment. It was almost like I was living out the things that happen to girls in romantic books and dramatic movies; things I'd never imagined would happen to me.

So much of the way we live online involves deception or trickery, whether it's taking liberties with our personalities through carefully composed About Me sections, or snapping photos from a flattering angle to cleverly disguise a double chin or scar – an act I was well versed in. If there's one thing *Catfish* reminds us of with nearly each episode, it's that fat people are much more likely to either hoax or be hoaxed online. When true identities are revealed over the threshold of sad people's homes, large bodies shout the answer to the unspoken question, 'Why did you do this?' As Margaret Lyons wrote on *Vulture* after the show's second season wrapped up, the stories on *Catfish* reinforce the damaging messages that instruct us not to become these pitiable people – the ones who are fat, poor and lonely – but if we do, to know that we should be ashamed and keep it a secret.

This is the trap that hopeful daters with low self-esteem and heavy bodies find themselves in: to be honest or to be loved.

'And while the show reminds us over and over that it's bad to lie,' Lyons wrote, 'it also subtly confirms that most of these people were right to: Nearly all of the catfishees, when confronted with the information that their catfishers were overweight, changed their tune about how in love they were.'

Telling this story has an added layer of humiliation; when Kathleen Kelly told Joe Fox that she only knew 'NY152' online, I doubt the unsaid explanation was *because there's no way a gorgeous man would fall for me in real life.*

When you're told your whole life that it's what's inside that counts and that your outside is not worth writing home about, online relationships seem like a godsend: they're a safe space where you can be sure that someone is getting to know you for who you are rather than just what you look like.

There's a horrifyingly astute fact that's pulled out time and again in stories like this, the one from *When Strangers Click*, HBO's 2011 documentary about online dating, the one about how women are afraid of meeting a serial killer, whereas men are afraid of meeting someone fat.

I felt lucky that Nate was paying me this much attention with all the attendant passion and drama hovering over it, and I convinced myself I loved him because he was the first person to pick me and tell me I was special, worth loving so hard. I am furious at him now, and protective of my sixteen-year-old self despite the fact that she should have known better. Deep down maybe she did, but being lied to by an internet lothario was still a new phenomenon in the mid 2000s, and not one that my friends (or people on reality TV) could empathise with. At the time, Mark Zuckerberg hadn't yet allowed non-university students to join 'thefacebook', your place in someone's Top 8 on Myspace was integral to the status of your relationship, and Catfish was just the name of the lake where Homer Simpson went to avoid marriage counselling. When I returned to school after that trip to Melbourne and told my friends and family I'd met the guy who kept calling and texting me, I was too embarrassed to say it hadn't happened outside a screen. I let them think he saw me before saying he loved me.

It's hard to believe, but all that was just establishing the scene of what would become an eighteen-month-long on-and-off exchange of thousands of words – so many of which I printed out, ordered chronologically and pasted into that scrapbook I still can't bring myself to toss out for the purposes of personal archiving. I've lost a lot of the details of Nate and the things we told each other in the decade since, but this trove helps me to piece it together. Because, even as a sixteen-year-old, I was anally retentive enough to date-stamp every piece of correspondence.

On 24 September 2006, Nate was quoting lyrics by my favourite band, Dashboard Confessional, and telling me, 'you know the real me, like no one else does'. Four days later, he tightened the cords that bound me to him:

> the things ive gone through with my health, has made me more aware of how precious life is. when i got rediagnosed 1 month ago, and when feelings for you got stronger, i realized there is not a minute i dont want to be with you.

Everything felt too heightened and dramatic; we chose every word so specifically and they all felt as heavy and fragile as glass. That same day, he wrote a letter to my mother that made my heart swell then, but now makes my blood boil. Like an olde-timey idiot, he assured her that he had 'only the purest and genuine intentions' and said, 'i hope in time, you'll see just how much love i hold in my heart for brodie.' (I've kept his messages verbatim here – including his inability to comprehend grammar and punctuation – because I am petty and bitter and it makes me feel better about myself and my ability to use a comma.) I proudly printed this out and gave it to my mum, who spent this entire time in my life quietly prompting me to think logically about what was happening, without barging in and bursting the bubble of hope I so desperately clung to.

I can now identify the threads of manipulation that kept me coming back for more. Nate told me that my friends and family didn't understand what we had, and that I didn't need them if I had him. He'd delete me from all his social networks, text me 'bye' and disappear for months. His six-month deadline came and went, but I never asked any questions and didn't notice when he stopped talking about chemotherapy.

What Nate wanted veered wildly, and like an obedient brides-maid kowtowing to a bridezilla, I would go along with his every whim. One day he was literally quoting *The Notebook* and telling me I was the reason he woke up in the morning; the next he was telling me to delete his phone number and stay out of his life. I was late to my Year 12 awards ceremony because he said he might hurt himself if I hung up the phone, so I sat there on the end of my bed, in my freshly ironed uniform and spit-polished black leather Mary Janes, while my family waited in the car for him to let me hang up. During the many periods in which we'd 'broken up' but still kept in constant contact, he would tell me about other girls he was seeing and what he did with them, then assure me he'd leave them and be with me when his health was better. He would hang up the phone if I tried to play along with the platonic friend game by mentioning other boys.

His story would change regularly and I silently and passively kept note of the edits. One day he'd be Straight Edge, the next he'd call me, say he was drunk, ask if I was a virgin and hang up after I told him yes. (Well, technically, I told him I'd done 'everything but', which was a straight-up lie – it had only been a few months since I'd had my first kiss and boob-touch – but his response was the same regardless.) He told me to stay home from school and talk to him on the phone instead. More than once he asked me to pay his phone bills, with the threat of not being able to call if he needed me hanging over my head if I said no – which I never did. When we first started talking, he spun stories about owning his own car and house and business, but I didn't remind him of that when I used my measly paycheck from my after-school job at Big W to keep him in contact with me. He sent me a poem he said he'd written for me (sample line: 'anywhere without you is not any kind of somewhere for me') and I suspiciously googled each line to see if it was plagiarised. My radar was on, I just ignored its beeping.

Unlike the people who email in stories just like this to Nev and Max on *Catfish*, I was never deeply invested in finding out who he really was in case it made him hang up the phone for good. The closest I came to uncovering any kind of truth was when I searched for the name of his band on Myspace and found it listed in just two results: one was on my own profile, the other was in the interests section of a profile belonging to a girl in Melbourne who had written blog posts about a boy with a sweet voice who made promises to meet her and never showed up. For once, I paid attention to my radar's deafening alarm. I reached out to her, knowing instinctively it was Nate, and she confirmed it when we shared the matching phone number of our respective ~mystery guys~. He used an entirely different name and profile when he made promises to her. This discovery came about during the long stretch of silence between the first time Nate said he loved me and the next time he contacted me, on my seventeenth birthday. He texted me that morning in January 2007, after months of nothing, telling me he would always love me. I spent the day at school trying not to cry and found myself

NO WAY! OKAY, FINE.

ready to believe him all over again, despite all logic and literal proof of his grand deception.

For a few months, we were back to where we started, only now he spoke about our relationship as if it had been forged by fire, as if we'd suffered through something real and survived, when really all that had happened was he had ignored me for a few months to concentrate on other gullible girls. 'I can't forgive myself for what I did, but it was a mistake,' one particularly dramatic message read, 'just know that the feelings were real, still are, im the one whos ruined, beyond comprehension.'

In May he declared that we'd get married 'once you turn eighteen, or nineteen, Depending on how long it takes me to earn enough money, To buy you the most amazing ring in this entire planet', but by July it was over forever. He sent me a text message that read, 'you're perfect for me, youre perfect in the way I need you to be, and to me that's all that matters'. Then he disappeared, forever this time. We never spoke again. He never knew me at age eighteen, let alone the person I'd become beyond that.

There was no context for what happened to me or how to handle it; when it was all over I just had to pretend nothing had happened. Mourning the break-up of such a falsified relationship didn't make sense, and I told myself the feelings I had developed were less legitimate because I had never held his hand or smelled his neck. No matter how much he lied and hurt me, I was in love with the idea of him, or of someone *like him* being so in love with me.

I compiled a playlist of all the songs he'd sent me or quoted in letters or told me reminded him of me, and played it on a loop that spring. The last song, 'Your Ex-Lover is Dead' by Stars, was one I'd recommended to him. I searched for the band's CDs in the local library (remember: dial-up internet) and saw that the track appeared on an album of the same name. Later on that same record was a song called 'He Lied About Death'.

A few months later, I graduated high school and at the party my classmates threw to celebrate our Year 12 formal, I kissed the boy I'd had a crush on before Nate appeared. Within three months of graduating, I'd moved to Melbourne for university, and spent my first year in the city going to gigs and parties with a girl I'd become friends with over Myspace because she, too, had been on the receiving end of Nate's compliments and lies. We'd sometimes wonder aloud if he was around, if he'd perhaps seen us together in public, riding trams or smoking outside a bar. He'd have the power then, too: it was unlikely we'd recognise him, or that the photos he used online were even of his own face, so he'd be able to know it was us, even get physically close to us, while we stayed clueless, as always.

After he stood her up on their first arranged meeting, Shopgirl wrote to NY152: 'The odd thing about this form of communication is you're more likely to talk about nothing than something. But I just want to say that all this nothing has meant more to me than so many somethings.' As sappy and gullible and naive as it makes me seem, that was the truth in my relationship with Nate. It wasn't healthy or right, but it meant something really real to me at a time when all I needed (but didn't know I needed) was attention and validation and someone who'd talk about nothing with me. It wasn't just his letters I kept; I archived my own as well. Reading back over one in particular, my heart breaks for the sixteen-year-old girl who wrote: 'I want you to see me and still be able to love me, like you promise you will and like no one's been able to do before.'

The trust I allowed myself to show Nate was hard earned and ultimately shattered, and in all the years since he exploited my vulnerability and shattered my hopes, I haven't been able to fully collect the pieces to try again. This formative relationship was opaque and disingenuous, and it gave me the opportunity to abandon logic and just listen to my silly heart that pounded in desperation. Ultimately and significantly, it was undone not by my gut and intuition, but by him calling the shots and deciding he was done.

I was not in control in this situation, but I didn't stop or question it. It was like when you're swimming in a pool and someone suggests starting a whirlpool, and before you know it you're running in a circle. At some point, your calves start to hurt but you can't stop because, even if you stopped running, the water would keep swirling around you. *Someone else might have suggested it*, you tell yourself, *but you didn't say no either*. Eventually, you all stop but the maelstrom doesn't; you're not in control, but it's a loss of control that you played a role in creating. Despite how much someone else's decisions and actions affected me without my consent, I couldn't shake the guilt over the contribution I made to my own emotional destruction.

When Kathleen and her boyfriend decide, mutually, to split up, he tells her he's developed feelings for a precocious TV host and asks if she's met someone else. Despite her feelings for NY152, she answers honestly: 'No, but there's the dream of someone else.' Maybe now that I've excavated and analysed my own dream of a person, I can close the book on this chapter of my life. Maybe the next time I move house, the scrapbook, that physical archive of an imaginary relationship, can be relegated to the throwaway pile. And maybe – hopefully – the next time I tell myself I'm too scared to make myself emotionally available, I'll remember how I got there once before, even if it was at the insistence of someone who never really existed.

CHAPTER 10

WHERE SHE'S ALLOWED

Women stop belonging to themselves the moment they decide to step outside their front doors. This is a fact as certain and true as the sun rising in the morning, or my period arriving the day after I wash my bedsheets. Once we begin to exist in the world, we become public property, like a bench or a street lamp or a bridge – except one with nice hair. Purely existing in public as a woman is an act of political performance.

When you are not a man, not a straight man, not a white man, not a man who has identified as a man from birth, everything you do in public is seen as being in service to them. When we unapologetically take up space, we are taking it away from them, when we wear make-up we are doing it for them, when we refuse to look cute, we are committing a personal offence to them. And they'll be sure to let us know.

In 2015, the internet's flavour of the week was a time-lapse video cataloguing a day's worth of catcalling one woman endured while walking the streets of Manhattan. Every woman watching could relate to her experience; I had used my headphones as a shield from things I could clearly hear through them enough times to know that when a man wants you to hear him he'll damn well make sure you do. I could relate to what that woman experienced and, judging by the millions of views on the video, and the number of days and weeks that articles about it appeared on my Facebook feed, I wasn't alone.

But soon enough, the feeling of understanding turned sour. Offshoot videos of 'boyfriends watching their girlfriends being catcalled', and 'fathers watching their daughters being catcalled', began cropping up, all of which once again reminded us that women's street harassment is more offensive to Their Men than to themselves. We see this when men are taught to sympathise with female victims of sexual assault because 'she is someone's wife or girlfriend or daughter or sister'. In every case, someone's = some man's. The fact that she is a person, a human in her own right, doesn't factor into this reasoning; a man's empathy for a violated woman is only generated once her relationship to another man is established. We saw it play out again after footage of Donald Trump and Billy Bush talking brazenly about assaulting unassuming women leaked during the 2016 election, and former supporters of the future president came out to meekly distance themselves from his actions with statements that always included the phrase, 'as a father'.

The comedian Aziz Ansari was applauded for an episode in his 2015 Netflix series *Master of None* that painted him as a feminist ally, one of the few guys who *gets it*. Titled 'Ladies and

Gentlemen', it opened with his character, Dev, feeling hard-done-by because a woman at the bar was served while the bartender ignored him. Meanwhile, his female co-worker Diana has to apologise for not throwing back a shot offered to her by a guy who winds up following her home from the same bar. The scene flits back and forth between Dev and his friend Arnold chatting about the weather on their walk home and taking a shortcut through a dark park, while Diana avoids men on the sidewalk by walking in the middle of the dimly lit street and dialling 9–1 on her phone so she can be ready to report the 'nice guy' who ultimately follows her into her apartment building with the press of the final 1.

As someone who's made a habit of walking home with her keys wedged between her knuckles, taking care to surreptitiously cross the street away from, or walk behind, any nearby men when I sense them in my periphery, it was exciting to see a very familiar scene like this play out on TV, but being told through the perspective of a male character like Dev made it frustratingly basic. The episode's female co-writers and director seem to feel the same, because while Dev tries to be empathetic, he never really *gets it*. How could he?

Diana tells Dev about her walk home when they arrive at work on Monday, and he then spends his next brunch quizzing his girlfriend, Rachel, and friend Denise on whether similar things have happened to them. Of course, they can readily list off their examples to Dev and Arnold. They know the things I know to be true, like how it feels to be sitting in a cab driven by a man who starts asking if you live alone, if you're single, why you're going home alone. They (and I) know how it feels to stay silent when you really want to say something, because the danger of speaking up is so great and the potential for that man to do or say whatever he likes is greater.

Arnold explains proudly that he's a feminist because, by definition, it means wanting men and women to be treated equally. With a straight face, Denise tells him she's impressed he knows that. I laughed at her response, before realising it wasn't being played for laughs; this was a scene in which a black gay woman effectively congratulates her white straight male friend – one who, while leaving the bar in the opening scene, said 'Girls are so annoying!' because the one he was trying to make out with left with another guy – for knowing the definition of a word.

Later, while riding the subway with Denise, Dev spots a guy jerking off. It's not an uncommon sight, but it's one that makes Dev want to change cars to avoid it. Denise insists they stay and do something about it; she's tired of just pretending shit like that isn't happening every day. They film him for evidence and make a citizen's arrest. Dev is on top of the world. Later at the bar he tells Diana and her friends about how he got the subway masturbator arrested and spends the night the hero; women are congratulating him, buying him shots, glad they're finally not complaining in a vacuum, despite the fact that Dev is only aware because Diana and Denise and Rachel have pried his eyes open by reminding him what their existence feels like. That same night, Dev downplays Rachel's insistence that his director friend, Brad Honeycut, exhibited clearly sexist behaviour by shaking hands with the men around her, while ignoring her presence.

Teaching men to be aware of the precautions women are forced to take in the world to feel even moderately more safe is an exhausting job that none of us signed up for, but even the quote-unquote nice guys like Dev and Arnold force us to assume the role and painstakingly detail how comparatively free they are to just exist, before inevitably doing what Dev does later, and minimising a display of seemingly innocuous misogyny when it's pointed out to him.

There is absolutely no doubt in my mind about whether or not these ideas are bred into us or if they're taught, even subconsciously, by the world. In her 2015 documentary *The Wolfpack*, director Crystal Moselle enters the New York City apartment of the Angulo siblings, six boys and a girl whose father has kept his wife and children hidden from the world their entire lives. One of the brothers, Mukunda, explains to Moselle's camera that some years would go by where they went outside nine times. One year, they never left at all. Their father implanted in them a fear of the world, of other people. The boys and their little sister were all home-schooled. They play instruments to an audience of no one, they re-enact their favourite films to inject a little magic into their routine. The boys never saw the world as a place where they had any control, as men seem to inherently understand when they've spent their entire life making the most of that privilege.

One Saturday morning in January 2010, the then fifteen-year-old Mukunda left the apartment wearing a mask he'd made to look like Michael Myers's from *Halloween*. He was picked up by the police, taken to hospital and given a therapist, whom his brothers were also instructed to visit regularly. Over time, the door began to open more often. The boys – who were now teenagers verging on men – started venturing out as a group. Dressed similarly to the characters they idolised in *Reservoir Dogs* – in suits, leather trenchcoats and Ray-Ban Wayfarers – with their waist-length black hair their father did not allow them to cut, they were at once trying to blend in and aware of every eye that was cast over them. Their reaction to being observed in the world was hyper familiar for women like me watching the film; the boys were nervous and careful, aware of their own safety and the potential of it disappearing with each step they took down the street. They were young men existing in public spaces full of men – ones designed for men – but unaware of the power they held there.

The structures that keep men safe and naive are the same ones that keep women on guard. During something like a moment of close-quarters catcalling – when a guy sits in the bus seat next to you, blocking your escape or he refuses to take 'no' for an answer in a pub and follows you every time you go to the bar alone – we often have to resort to the line, 'I have a boyfriend.' It might be a lie, but it feels safer than 'I'm not interested.' Even before I knew why I was saying it, why men seemed genetically and biologically and sociologically predisposed to accept another man's claim on a woman more readily than that woman's disinterest in them, I knew it was the tool in my arsenal that would protect me more than any other.

Because, the fact is, being disinterested or a stranger or too young or at work doesn't stop anyone from taking from you what they want.

I was filled with fury when I saw you from behind in class that day, sliding your hand up my friend's leg as she sat, frozen, next to you, afraid to react and disturb the lesson. We were only thirteen but you were tall for your age and as broad as a truck. No one could've fought back against you even if they'd been brave enough. When I tried to bring it up later – playing the part of the cool, casual girl, all the while terrified that saying something against you would threaten my already precarious place in the high school hierarchy – you pushed your hard chest into mine, standing so close I could see the abscesses of your acne and smell your curdled breath as you hissed, 'The only good thing about how fat you are is that you've got those huge tits.' The next year, during a fight with my sister after I'd embarrassed her in front of her friends, she'd scream at me and demand to know why I couldn't be cool like you.

When you invite me over to your house on school holidays to catch up and when I ask if I can bring anything and you say 'condoms lol' I should've known, right? I should've known when you said you wanted to look at my new iPod and, when I got close enough to show you, you pulled me onto your lap. I should've known when you asked if the boy I'd recently kissed – the one I'd shared my first kiss with – had 'snatched my V-card' that you had a reason for asking. I tossed away the suspicion because your mother had spent years telling me I was the daughter she'd never had and I didn't realise it was possible to feel so unsafe in your house. When I left, I made an excuse. 'My sister just told me she's at her friend's house around the corner! What a coincidence! I'll be right back!' The truth didn't feel safe and so it wasn't an option. When I saw you on the first day of school the next year, the story had changed. The new narrative was that I was desperate for you and had invented the whole story.

I thought I imagined it when you grabbed my butt because even though I felt the phantom pinch days later, by the time

I'd turned around you were swallowed into a crowd. You were anonymous, a ghost, but blessed with the ability to make me feel repulsed. If the way you spend New Year's Eve is the way you'll spend the rest of the year, then that year would be one filled with shame and shock and humiliation.

I was the journalist interviewing your band when you lingered by my shoulder as I got cash out of an ATM. I was still doing my job when I showed up at the bar your publicist invited me to after the show and you yelled, 'She came!!' to your friends and bandmates. I pretended I was still professional when you leaned so close that I could've guessed the temperature of your breath with absolute certainty to whisper that Australians (like me) and Californians (like you) are a lot alike, convincing me of our compatibility. I wasn't doing my job when you saw me going to the bathroom and pulled me against you in a dark corner, saying how glad you were that it was me who was sent to cover your show. Or when, the next day, you accepted my Facebook friend request and I saw you'd had a girlfriend all along. I felt like I'd invented it all, or that I was the unfit competitor running through the instant replay of your game, searching for the tactical manoeuvres that should've tipped me off, but didn't.

I keep a running log in my head of every moment my safety and humanity has been compromised because I've dared to exist in the world. I keep a list so that, when a friend summons the courage to bring up one of their examples, I can relate; or if a broken woman becomes another headline and the tone is disbelieving, as though her trauma is the exception and not the rule, I can pull from my own arsenal to prove that her life is our lives, desperately hoping that one more anecdote about routinely and automatically texting a friend the ID number of a taxi driver whose car you sit in will make them realise that these are not one-off experiences shared only by girls who put themselves at risk.

But after a certain point, the list gets too long. The week I wrote this chapter, Australian news has blown up with reports of schoolboys sharing explicit photos and videos of their female classmates. The news has been met by conservative commentators and pseudo-feminist mouthpieces with clutched pearls and warnings for girls to just stop sexting or taking intimate photos. The fact that some photos were taken while the girls slept or showered, without their consent, has largely gone unacknowledged. Educators at girls' schools around the country are pulling female students into modesty lectures and policing the lengths of their skirts as their male classmates are allowed to stay in class. Meanwhile, on a beach in Nice, a Muslim woman is forced by police to remove her 'Burkini' – a swimsuit invented by Sydney designer Aheda Zanetti to allow women wearing the hijab to swim and participate in water sports – as onlookers cheered and her daughter cried. Meanwhile, a seventeen-year-old Welsh student who posted a photo of her new headphones on Snapchat received a reply from a stranger saying, 'You wearing those, and nothing else, that would be heaven.' Screenshots of the original image and the response went viral on Twitter with the ironic caption, 'Boys wouldn't send weird messages if you didn't put up such slutty photos.'

The emotional hard drive is full, because no matter how 'right' or 'good' we are, there is always something wrong and someone to remind us our safety is never assured. There are just too many lingering touches, or puffs of hot rum breath on your neck, or hands of the person you're enjoying kissing straying from your face and creeping up to the top of your head to push you down a little too roughly like he's trying to drown you, or bus trips spent deliberately ignoring the person talking about you, their leg pressing against yours, their voice growing louder as if daring you to acknowledge that you can hear him over the music in your headphones. There are too many examples for each one of us that, if we dared to add them all up, they would overwhelm us all. We pick the ones to yell about, but ignore most of them. Not because they don't matter, not because they don't leave welts, but because reacting to every heckle or grab or press of a body would mean we'd never get anything else done.

I was born in the first month of the '90s, on the eve of Riot Grrrl, the punk movement that would go on to exemplify how women used their defiant voices and demeaned bodies to make powerful statements in music. The first time I listened to Bikini Kill almost two decades later and heard Kathleen Hanna, the band's ferocious singer and the recalcitrant face of the Riot Grrrl movement, her voice sounded like a volcano. It was urgent, with the potential to ignite fiery destruction.

Kathleen knew her body was political. Instead of shying away from or resenting it, though, she mobilised around it. She scrawled the word SLUT on her belly when she wasn't wearing a top, and eschewed pants when she was; she sang songs to and about the men who touched and looked at and commented on her flesh. The song 'White Boy' is about the patriarchal demands put on women: to lie back and take it, and then to shut up about how much it hurts. It opens with audio of Kathleen talking to a man, the titular white boy, his backwards baseball cap invisible but inferred. He says he can't possibly be blamed for what he does to women, because, no matter how hard they deny it, the way they dress when they walk down the street tells him they 'want it'. Little has changed in the world since that song was recorded. I've lived every year of my life with those sentiments. We all have.

After the dissolution of Bikini Kill, Kathleen engaged in a less-public approach to music making, discovering the world of DIY samples and loops that would lead her to craft a self-titled record under the name The Julie Ruin in 1998. 'Bedroom producer' is a descriptor usually attached to men making independent dance music on their computers. Their unseen work is enigmatic and heralded. Girls' bedrooms, comparatively, are imagined as being flowery and intimate, the place for whispered conversations and confessional diary-writing. Kathleen's work straddled both worlds, and the important part about what she was doing in the late '90s was the place where it all happened. In *The Punk Singer*, the 2013 documentary about her life and work, she said she wanted this record to sound like it was made by a girl in her bedroom, but instead of throwing it away or keeping it secret – like so many things birthed in that safe and protected space are – it was shared with the world.

The record is rich with Kathleen's signature combination of poetry and political activism, peppered with love songs for her husband, Adam Horovitz of the Beastie Boys. But its centrepiece is 'I Wanna Know What Love Is', a chilling meditation on the price women pay for just existing. She confronts the police force's history of racial discrimination and the lack of attention or importance placed on the murder and abuse and dehumanisation of women. Surrounding these interrogations of what we accept as 'just the way things are' are the samples Kathleen taught herself to weave using a cheap drum machine, including a loop from the Clash's 'Guns of Brixton' and her own voice mimicking Foreigner's original titular plea to know what love is. *Nowhere is safe*, Kathleen seems to be reminding me in this song, *not your love or your activism or your relationships or your law enforcement.* Her final verse describes the weaponised approach she takes to going to bed at night: staying awake, a pen in one hand, a knife in the other.

Like so many university students in their early twenties, I went through a phase of obsession with the film *Into the Wild*, and the book by Jon Krakauer on which it was based. The idea of abandoning the trappings of a consumerist life like the story's hero, Christopher McCandless, did in 1990 seemed liberating and exciting and possible. In the film, McCandless (played by Emile Hirsch) hitchhikes across America, stopping to stay in welcoming, Burning Man-esque desert cities on his romantic journey to nowhere. He eschews the conventions of society that had been imposed upon him by his recently completed Ivy League education and supportive parents to dig deep into the ideals of independence and inherent goodness espoused by transcendentalism. McCandless was carefree and cocky, two traits that led him to shed the remainder of his sparse possessions as he ventured into the Alaskan wilderness in winter. It was there that, Krakauer hypothesised, he'd consume the seeds of an Alaskan potato that his lean, malnourished body couldn't digest. His body was found five months later, inside the abandoned bus he'd been living in for the 100-odd days before his death.

Cheryl Strayed did not have the same hubris. When she set out to walk the Pacific Crest Trail, between the Mojave Desert and the Oregon–Washington border, she was prepared. She had the boots, the backpack, the books and the deep emotional suffering she hoped the walk would help her to exorcise or accept. In her book, *Wild*, and the 2014 film adaptation of the same name, Cheryl is cautious and headstrong. She has anticipated changes in weather and terrain; she has planned rest stops and keeps her family informed of her whereabouts. Despite the defiance of Mother Nature, Cheryl feels she's in control. But there is one factor she cannot influence or plan for, and that is the existence of men in her path.

Cheryl's journey can be divided into three sections: the past, the present and the future. The past is her reason for attempting the trek in the first place; it is her *why*. The past is where her beloved mother died of cancer, it's where she used heroin and cheated on her husband with a man who impregnated her. It's where she got an abortion and hoped for her husband's forgiveness. The present is the ground under her feet, the air around her head, the blisters on her heels, the songs and poetry in her memory, and the fox – a spiritual symbol of her mother – that appears incrementally along the journey and guides her along. The future is men, and their presence implants a question mark into her plan. When a man picks her up in his truck, he seems threatening and her safety becomes immediately uncertain. He asks too many questions, looks for too long. He is a farmer, and takes Cheryl home where his wife cooks dinner for her. Even then, in the certainty of a home, safety is never guaranteed. A pair of hunters is an even more direct threat to Cheryl. They first appear when she is dehydrated and desperate and particularly vulnerable, and describe what they'd like to do to her loudly enough to send waves of silent fear coursing through her veins.

There are some similarities in the stories of Christopher McCandless and Cheryl Strayed. Both are white Americans who embarked on gruelling physical and spiritual treks to escape something in their past and cleanse themselves of their family's expectations of them. The differences, though, cannot be denied. Where Cheryl was prepared and well researched, McCandless was content to wing it; his physical and sexual safety was implied by default of his gender, whereas Cheryl's femaleness made her a target. The idea of finding spiritual salvation or emotional freedom by leaving your safety net of people and warmth and roofs behind is one that is assured for men, while a woman in the wild is inherently at risk.

But a woman doesn't need to be isolated in the forest to be threatened by the proximity of men socialised to see us as potential conquests. They can feel entitled to photograph or film us on public transport without fear of repercussions; we were there, we were to blame. They can gleefully orchestrate web-wide harassment campaigns against any one of us who expresses an opinion with which they disagree; serves us right for being mouthy, we knew what we were getting into. Teenage girls are being sent home from school because their visible knees and midriffs might be too distracting for their male classmates, while those boys will grow up to tear off their shirts the second the mercury hits 25, no matter the public location, safe in the knowledge that no harm will come to them. When Stanford university student Brock Turner raped an unconscious girl at a party, he was sentenced to just a few months in prison – a sentence his father said, in a statement he read to the open court in 2016, was 'a steep price to pay for 20 minutes of action out of his 20 plus years of life'.

Our bodies are treated as public property that anyone is allowed to comment on or object to or destroy. We can't be mad when that happens; purely by existing we're asking for it.

Kim Kardashian West built a career up from the foundation of her face and butt. Her body is a commodity, and seeing it all as she licked and kissed and sucked brought her to the world's attention a decade ago – but since that sex tape, her body has never been something that she allowed the world to consume or use without her explicit consent.

After stepping off a sixteen-hour flight to Los Angeles in March 2016, I was trying desperately to keep up with the Kardashians' latest Twitter row over what a wife and mother should do with her body. (You know, one of those cool convos the internet loves to have?!) Who knows how many Kardashian scandals or dramas will have taken place between me writing this and you reading it, so lemme catch you up on what I'm referring to: Kim tweeted an image of her naked body (with black bars running across her chest and pelvis) that she'd taken in the mirror.

Anyone with eyes and a photographic memory of every style choice she makes (ie me) could tell you it was not a recent picture. If you've studied hard enough it is possible to tell time in terms of a Kardashian's appearance, like counting the rings of a tree or waiting for light to pass over a sundial. Kim's cropped, peroxide-blonde hair in the photo tells you it was clearly taken in the first or second week of March 2015, when she bleached her hair during Paris Fashion Week – ie a time between giving birth to her daughter, North, and announcing her pregnancy with her son, Saint. No one wanted to talk about the photo's year-old timestamp, though – rather, the conversation flitted from what a wife and mother is allowed to do with her body to the fragility of the concept of being empowered by nudity, as Kim said she is.

Kim's career is her body, and her day job is her life. She is filmed around the clock for US cable channel E!'s landmark reality TV show *Keeping Up With the Kardashians*, and when the cameras stop, her phone comes on. She Snapchats and tweets and invites us in, but only to the parts of her she wants us to see. Living online means living in public – this is true for all of us – but Kim is the first to remind you that the choice to live in public does not come coupled with an implied allowance to cut off a piece of her image and use it however you want.

When actor Chloë Grace Moretz tweeted, '@KimKardashian I truly hope you realize how important setting goals are for young women, teaching them we have so much more to offer than just our bodies', all she did was show her own narrow-mindedness; the idea that displays of nudity or public vanity or – as Kim did – both at once somehow rule out the possibility of someone also engaging in goal-setting or personal determination is backwards and outdated. It was a reminder that Kim can be both an exhibitionist and a smart, successful woman; a reminder that it's not just men who will assume you're either one or the other based on the height of your hemline or visibility of your nipples.

By October that year, the ground under Kim had shifted impermeably. Her social media fell silent during another trip to Paris Fashion Week and she wouldn't post on it again for four months. Alone in her hotel room, Kim was held up by two armed men dressed as police officers. Bound and gagged, she feared for her life as the men made off with an estimated $10 million in jewellery, including a ring her husband, Kanye West, had recently gifted her. He was informed of the news while performing in New York, and left the stage. Almost instantly, wheels of doubt and conspiracy started turning: had she set it up as a publicity ploy? Perhaps as a way to trade on sympathy? Was Kanye in on it? Whoever was behind it, skeptics agreed on one thing: it was all Kim's fault. Her privacy might have been invaded, she may have been traumatised and feared she'd never see her children again, but she was the one who broadcast her life to the world. She deserved what she got because she posted images of the diamond ring on social media. Even her friends in the fashion industry, people like Karl Lagerfeld, who trades in luxury and exclusivity, were quick to point the finger at Kim for her garish displays of wealth.

When we're surrounded by tabloid outlets that say a woman wearing leggings is 'flaunting' her curves and people view a woman alone in her hotel room as someone begging to be robbed, what safety can the rest of us rely on? We're not ours when we're in the world. The same people who pay hundreds of tax-deductible dollars to sit in musty conference rooms learning how to make their personal brands more valuable will also gleefully dive into the comments section of any article with 'Kardashian' in the title to say *Who cares?!* and *This is not news!* and *There are children starving in Africa!* and *Girls have negative body image and she's responsible because she's taking her clothes off!* and *She's a mother – how dare she?!* If we're to tune into this white noise, it will tell us that Kim deserved to be robbed, and the rest of us deserve what we get too.

I never realised how on guard my body was until I had to literally pay for it in physiotherapy bills. What I assumed was an injury resulting from sitting at a desk, staring at a screen, writing these words with few breaks in between, was actually the result of over-correcting, of standing at attention, bracing my knees and puffing out my chest. I felt my desperation to not appear meek in the back spasms that my impacted muscles endured each time I drew breath. I am subconsciously contorting my body to give the illusion of bravery, but the literal physical pain it causes proves it is no more than a masquerade of bravado.

Every time I adjust my posture I am trying to grasp onto a little control of how it's perceived, but it's ultimately a pointless effort. It wasn't until I started getting tattoos on my arms that I realised what a barrier they created between me and the people who would potentially enter my space, and the potential for safety they offer. I'm watched or commented on or leered at so much more often in winter – or if I throw on a jacket – when the ink is hidden. In a strange reversal of what I'd always known, when my skin is on display now, I feel more protected than ever. No matter how deceptive it might be, I seem at least a little unfuckwithable when my tattoos are visible.

'There is a scene with Cheryl and a trucker,' I wrote in my journal, weeks after seeing *Wild*, finding myself unable to shake it. 'It's all about the choice to quit or keep going. You can only quit if you reach a dead end, when there's no fork in the road offering you any choice between two (or more) possibilities. Going down one straight road is also a choice, in a way – the choice to keep plodding along, knowing your goal is signposted along the way. Since seeing the movie, I haven't been able to decide if I'd prefer being on that straight road over the one I'm on now, one that gets twistier every day.'

There is no easy answer to ensure our survival. The route to it is hidden. It's dangerous terrain, with possible paths and potential threats splintering off the route at every turn. Some of those paths will be unsafe, some of them will lead to truckers you read as threatening who really just want to feed you and make sure you're warm. Not to get all #NotAllPaths or #NotAllTruckers, but I know the solution isn't to allow myself to trust everyone in the hope that my trust will be rewarded, just as the approach of treating all situations and people with caution isn't an effective one. There is no right answer. All I can do is listen to my gut, trust in my instincts, rely on my fear, wear comfortable shoes and believe in women when they tell me what they know or have seen. That's all the hope we can have.

CHAPTER 11

BODY LIKE VELVET

I was twelve the first time a boy broke up with me for being fat. It would happen dozens more times in different, less direct ways after that, but this message – told to his friend who told it to my friend who told it to me, as these things go when you're a literal child – was loud and clear and never quite stopped echoing in my head. As I grew older it became men, not boys, telling me, only they didn't so much *tell me* as they *let me know*. The first time it happened, I was devastated. The second time, I was sad and disappointed. The more often it happened, the less surprised I became until I reached the point of numbness. It was clear that the way I looked kept me from being girlfriend material.

In the Venn diagram of 'fatophobes' and 'garden-variety misogynists', my dating life exists in the intersection. You don't realise quite how pervasive ideas about fat women and sex are until you receive your first OKCupid message about how grateful you should be for attention, or one presuming you're an expert at giving blowjobs because (I have to assume) you're a) always stuffing something in your mouth and b) desperate to please anyone who will deign to give you attention.

Although that's not always the stereotype: Kim Kardashian West once referred to her sister Khloe as 'Khloe Blowie' on *Keeping Up with the Kardashians*, prompting the youngest Kardashian daughter to explain that was the nickname of a different Chloe in their high school – it should've been obvious, she said, because she was 'the fat one' in high school and nobody would want to get a blowjob from a fat girl. After saying proudly that being fat saved her from 'being a whore in life' – a truly offensive declaration that only served to reinforce the assumption that her body size is directly linked to her ability to be loved – Khloe continued to explain that she respected her ex-husband Lamar Odom because he loved her before she famously lost a lot of weight. I hated hearing these words, but it's not like I've never thought the same things myself in the deepest and saddest parts of myself. The world tells us that fat women are not the people you should aspire to love, and – if you happen to be one – to feel grateful that someone would ever dare to pay you romantic or sexual attention. We're built to believe that our flesh and bones are regretful detours on the road to someone better (thinner). We are the things your friends will roast you about. Despite knowing how fucked up that expectation is, I'd be lying if I said it didn't filter into my mind when someone noticed me.

The bulk of my romantic experience as an adult has been with either chubby chasers who go out of their way to let me know they like me for my body alone, or men who resent their attraction to it then use it as an excuse to dip out. The former seem to think they're being smooth, that they are more mature and open-minded than the men who don't see the same potential in my flesh, when they steer a perfectly pleasant conversation to the line that's always a dead giveaway: 'You know, I like bigger girls.' I'm never brave enough to spit back a sassy line about how that's not a special achievement; usually I just go with a lie, like, 'So does my boyfriend.' I can't tell if the skepticism I see on their face is in my imagination or not.

The 2003 documentary *Fat Girls and Feeders* was my first exposure to the culture of fetishisation that exists around fat women's bodies. It follows a couple – Mark, a feeder, and his wife Gina, his project – as they explore the concept of BBW (Big Beautiful Women) empowerment in the context of online porn. I had never seen a woman with a body like Gina's eroticised in such a way, and at first the possibility of what that meant was freeing and exciting. As the camera pans over the rolls of fat surrounding her bones, Gina describes what turns on the men who pay to watch her videos online, and purrs that her body must feel luxurious to them, like velvet. But while the possibility of being attractive and loved at any size felt free, the reality was the opposite: Gina was trapped inside a body that Mark controlled, as he urged her to get bigger to satisfy his seemingly never-ending erotic aspirations. He was aroused by her mass and wanted to be the one who enlarged it and got to touch it, while his likeminded community online could only look. She was his creation, and there was nothing admirable about the way he treated her body; coveting and eroticising bigness makes a person no more respectable than those who actively avoid it.

Being approached by a fetishist doesn't make me feel excited or grateful or confident. The first time it happened I realised that feeling of being actively wanted for my body was one I hadn't experienced since the school sports carnival where people fought over whose tug-o-war team I'd be on because I was sturdy and strong. But being wanted only because you're big doesn't feel much better than being rejected for the same reason. And the more often it happens, the louder the voice grows in my head suggesting I just relent and say yes. It's the same voice that asks if it really matters *why* someone likes you when they do at all.

I know I'll sound like a broken record when I say, again, that the rules are different for men and women . . . but the rules are different for men and women, especially when those rules are written on our bodies. There is no rhyming nickname given to a man's tattoo placement that suggests his level of 'trampiness'; we've seen enough pairings of portly men and their thin wives on sitcoms to last a lifetime; when a woman feels even a suggestion of being friend-zoned by someone she has a crush on, she's likely to see it as a reflection of some personal failing, whereas men who expect (or even demand) intimacy from the women they're interested in, blame those women for not returning their affection. Sometimes, like in the case of Fran on *Girls* when Hannah called off their relationship, they loudly curse out the dumb bitch who dared to dump such a nice guy; in the case of Elliot Rodger – the 22-year-old student in California who posted YouTube videos claiming to be 'the perfect guy' and 'a supreme gentleman' – he decided retribution for rejection would come after he murdered classmates and passers-by as revenge for the unnamed women who weren't interested in him.

For the record, I think the friend zone is a bullshit notion. It suggests that we all enter public spaces and platonic relationships expecting to be lusted over and, when that doesn't happen, put the blame on the person who didn't play by the unspoken rules. I don't think friendship is a punishment – nor that romantic rejection is a crime – but I also don't know a word that so succinctly communicates the feeling of *oh no, you read this* all *wrong* quite like it.

The intersection of the friend zone and the slippery, rocky landscape of being a fat woman with desires is front and centre in a scene in the Paul Feig-directed movie *Spy*. Susan Cooper, played by my guardian angel Melissa McCarthy, is sharing a meal with her CIA partner Bradley Fine (Jude Law at his most smarmy and James Bond-iest) after she singlehandedly helped him to escape a dangerous mission. He sends her a stream of clear signals – both at this dinner and during their missions, as she watches remotely and feeds him solutions via an earpiece. He tells her she's the best and wonders aloud, 'What would I do without you?' (The answer to which, by the way, is, 'Die. You would literally just be dead without her.')

Sure, he's an amalgam of all charming British spies in films – he's being chased by a team of dudes with rifles and has no means of escape, but still manages to flirt with women – but he shows Susan genuine, intimate affection and appreciation. She is full of compliments for him, and when she insults herself, he stops her – if only to reinforce their power dynamic – and reminds her that the two of them make a perfect team. So, when he tells her he couldn't do what he does without her, and presents her with a velvet box, she's not delusional for imagining that her fantasy has come to life. That is, until she opens the box and sees the plastic necklace in the shape of a 'crazy cupcake' inside. 'Imagine how awkward it would've been if it had been a diamond ring or something,' he laughs, crushing her fantasy and reinforcing the platonic boundary with one throwaway line. Imagine. *Crazy.*

Of course he's not interested, Susan berates herself afterwards; of course when he said that he *could* kiss her, he never actually wanted to; of course it's because of who you are, inherently and as a person, that this man cannot love you. I can empathise with Susan; I've got the text messages telling me what an amazing woman I am and how lucky someone would be to be with me, sent by people with no interest in being that person, to prove it. There is safety in that kind of expression; you don't need to make yourself vulnerable or brace for rejection when you don't see the person receiving your affection as any kind of option. I've spent hours getting ready for dates I arranged – ones where I made sure to use the word 'date' in the text message or email just to make certain that, *this time*, they'd know for sure what I was really asking – and shown up to find my date had invited a friend along. I've sat listening to my guy friends describing the most *amazing, gorgeous* women they just met and wondering aloud when they'll get a chance to get to know her better, after which I go home alone wondering if getting to know who I am will ever make someone think I'm beautiful and worth pursuing in the same way. I've heard coupled-up friends talk about how eager they are to matchmake their *amazing* single friend with a nice girl, heard them cycling through and weighing up every possible option, oblivious to my presence. When you've never been seen as an option, when you watch season after season of dating shows like *The Bachelor* and never see someone who looks like you in the line-up of possible romantic options, it can feel like you're going mad with these thoughts, like the world sees you in totally opposing terms to those in which you see yourself – as worthy, loveable and beautiful not despite or because of your body.

I have friends with bodies that look like mine who have had a wealth of healthy and encouraging and fortifying sexual and romantic relationships, so I'm not saying it's not possible. If anything, the existence of those bonds only makes my experience more frustrating and my radar less effective. I am comically unable to notice flirting, even if it's happening to me. I'm so unaccustomed to being the focus of romantic attention that, when I am, I'm like a naive ditz from a teen rom-com who ~can't see what's been in front of her all along~ because someone took her prescription glasses away in a makeover scene. (I'm mixing my *She's All That* and *Can't Hardly Wait* analogies, but you get it.) More than anything else, this situation makes me feel alone, like the only person thinking and feeling these things.

But I'm not. I know that because of TV (what else?). On an episode of *Louie* in 2014, Louis CK's differently spelled titular character meets a fat woman called Vanessa, played by Sarah Baker, who is his waitress at a bar before she assertively asks him out and makes her intentions perfectly clear. He is thrown, and turns her down initially. When he eventually agrees to go out with her, she offhandedly mentions her body in a matter-of-fact way, and he does the thing that men who are trying really hard not to make A Big Deal out of something do: he downplays it to the point of showing just what A Big Deal it is to him. She calls him on it, telling him how disappointing it is for him to pretend not to notice she's fat, and calling out the double standards at play in the ways that men and women talk about their bodies. Louie can talk about how he's overweight and can't get a date in his stand-up act and be adored, she says, but if she were to express the same complaint, she'd be pitied. People would be concerned about her emotional stability.

'Can I just say it? . . . It sucks to be a fat girl,' Vanessa exasperatedly tells Louie.

> On behalf of all the fat girls, I'm making you represent all the guys. Why do you hate us so much? What is it about the basics of human happiness, feeling attractive, feeling loved, having guys chase after us, that's just not in the cards for us? . . . How is that fair? And why am I supposed to just accept it?

I don't entirely agree with Vanessa telling Louie that 'it sucks to be a fat girl' – I learned the tools long ago that have helped me to love my body and directed me away from blaming it for the everyday effects of a thinness-obsessed culture that trades in shame and self-hate. I do, however, understand what she was saying: it sucks to be a fat girl trying to be loved in a world full of people who can't comprehend that you could possibly deserve it.

What follows is the greatest truth I've ever seen play out on a TV comedy: Vanessa calls Louie on his own insecurities that keep him from flirting back with her, forcing him to confront what it is about himself that makes him so terrified to be seen with someone like her. The really classically hot guys she flirts with? They have no problem returning the affection. The Bradley Fines of the world, those 'high-calibre studs', are confident enough in themselves to flirt with the Vanessas or Susans because they themselves are constantly reminded of their physical worth and being seen charming a fat woman wouldn't diminish that. But the men like Louie, Vanessa says, the men who prove the adage about loving yourself before you can love anyone else, they find the things they hate about themselves and project them onto Vanessa/Susan/me until the very sight of us fills them with self-loathing. When they don't flirt back, it's as if destroying that sexual confidence in us will destroy that part of themselves that tells them they don't deserve more than us.

The viciousness that is inspired by a classically hot man desiring any woman bigger than a Victoria's Secret angel is real and red hot. When HBO aired an episode of *Girls* called 'One Man's Trash' in 2013 we were all prodded and burned by it. In the episode, Hannah, played by the show's creator Lena Dunham, spends a weekend fucking and playing half-nude ping pong with a hot, recently separated older man in his dope brownstone. Even before *Girls* premiered, Lena's body made people vocally angry because she was naked on TV, sometimes in non-sexual contexts, while daring not to be thin in the process. So, of course, the casting of certified dreamboat Patrick Wilson as this episode's love interest further stoked the flame. In *Esquire*'s recap, they compared the tenuous reality of the episode to one of *The Cosby Show* where Cliff Huxtable dreamed that he and his male sons were pregnant. 'This week's *Girls* was a lot like that *Cosby Show*,' Peter Martin wrote, 'except Hannah never woke up from the fantastical, implausible story she found herself in.'

I didn't think it was possible for the volume of conversations about Lena Dunham's body to increase, but that episode dug up all of our assumptions about the romantic viability of women and dumped them on the table in front of us. The very notion of someone who looked like Patrick Wilson wanting to stick his dick in, let alone have intimate and quiet sex, unlike any we've seen on this show, with someone who looks like Hannah Horvath – a character who once inanely announced that she was 'twelve pounds overweight and it has been a struggle for me my entire life!' (and who, I should mention, is at least four or five dress sizes smaller than I am) – was so incredibly unbelievable. The general consensus was to dissect her body, to tear it to bits like a premature autopsy and examine her soft, round belly and legs that rub together at the top to try to find the answer to how she possibly tricked him into it.

Shortly after that episode of *Louie* aired, my favourite advice columnist Heather Havrilesky, who answers the 'Ask Polly' questions on *The Cut*, was asked the question, 'Do I Have to Lose Weight to Find Love?' from a woman who was tired of ignoring her body in the hopes that someone would love her for all her charms and non-visible attributes.

She gave voice to my fears about loneliness, and my desire to be loved for my most special components – a fantasy in which my body becomes neither an afterthought nor the sole appeal, but rather just the thing that holds the rest of me. I've written at length about how desperately I needed to see my reality reflected back at me from my screens, but now that it was – via Vanessa's monologue on *Louie*, which this letter writer admitted to not having the stomach to watch for fear of how closely it would align with her own experience – it was almost too real and too scary; the 'me too!'-ness I usually crave was replaced by the fear of how close to the bone it cut.

In her reply, Heather admitted to understanding the pain, while also admitting that she could never truly understand it herself. 'I have a plus-size friend who tells me there is nothing – NOTHING – like showing up for an online date and reading on the guy's face, "Oh, you're too big for me." She tells me I can't possibly know a thing about that feeling, and I trust that she's right.'

Online dating has the potential to feel like a gift, because it both gives me the opportunity to control how people see me, and offers a type of protection in the form of a 'Block' button if they make it aggressively clear that they don't like what they see. Because even for all its benefits, it's not safe from the types of men who can't help but tell you what they think of your body. I've been in an on-again-off-again relationship with OKCupid for many years, but during my most recent (and, safe to say, final) time venturing into its murky waters, the responses I got to the smallest details on my profile clarified everything I knew to be true about strange men and the way they saw my body. My username on the site was couchfan69 – a lazy attempt to come up with something silly and dumb at a time when I was filled with resentment and disbelief over signing up for this shit *again* – and in the 'body type' section I used the default drop-down options to describe myself as 'five-foot-ten' (true) and 'jacked' (a joke). On the day I decided to close down my account, after months and months of creepy dudes asking about my feet and seemingly decent dudes ignoring my messages, I got two inbox notifications that propelled me to shut that shit down for good. The first read, 'no offence, but you look like you're a fan of sitting on a couch.'

The second was from a man in America who, it turned out, trawled the site for women who categorised themselves using the options 'overweight', 'a little extra', 'curvy' or 'full figured'. He was mad at me for making him work harder to find my profile by not using those descriptors and signed off, 'FYI, your body type is closer to "full figured" than "jacked" as "jacked" implies that you have a bodybuilder's body'.

These drop-down options are a contentious issue, particularly for people who don't feel the need to sugarcoat their own descriptions of their body. I would have much rather described myself as 'fat' than OKCupid's softly, softly option: 'curvy'.

While researching for this chapter, I discovered a post on the OKCupid subreddit where a male user translated all the possible options we can use to categorise our body types on the site. The user's reading of them, tellingly, only applied to cisgender women. He began by breaking down what the options *should* mean:

Curvy = hourglass shape, thin waist with ample bosom and
    buttocks
A little extra = some trouble spots, but well short of obese
Full figured = chubby
Average = not skinny, not fat, no real curves to speak of.

It was clear that, in his estimation, only the first and fourth options were acceptable, and any woman who identified or met the criteria of the middle two options was to be avoided. In this reading, 'chubby' is a four-letter word. Below this ranking he wrote what these options more commonly mean on OKCupid: fat, fat, fat, fat.

To add insult to injury, he also warned that the pictures you choose should make you look good, but not *too* good; if you present yourself in too flattering a light, all you'll do is disappoint people.

In the Christmas special of BBC's *The Office*, Ricky Gervais's character David Brent meets a woman called Susan he's been talking to online, and is instantly unimpressed with her because of the way she looks – perhaps fifteen kilos and a few years older than she was in her photo. Even worse, he is horrified that she's not entertaining him to over-compensate for her looks, and pathetically explains to the camera, 'I thought she'd be one of them, sort of, happy, bubbly ones 'cause of her eating. She's, blergh, nothin'.' Granted, Brent is an awful character who regularly and spectacularly puts his foot in his mouth, but his expectation of her to perform and amuse him as penance for her appearance speaks to something more insidious. In the minefield of being a fat woman trying to date online, you never know what transgression will set off an explosion: you're not open about your fatness and you try to disguise it only to be found out later; you're too bawdy and take pleasure in being the focus of attention (*how dare you have that confidence*); or you don't satisfy a quota of being jolly and entertaining, like a bumbling clown, willing to humiliate yourself for someone's entertainment.

A comedian called Mike Faverman came under fire in 2016 for his horrifyingly sexist and body-shaming messages to a woman he had met IRL and decided would be grateful for his attention. He asked her, 'When am I taking you to dinner?' To which she replied, 'I'm sorry if [I] gave you the impression that I wanted to date you by becoming your [Facebook] friend . . . That wasn't my intention.' That directness spoke of confidence he didn't think she was allowed, and it made him mad. 'You have to remember I met you. So I know you're not out of my league in the least, please stop acting as if I wouldn't have a chance,' he fired back at her polite refusal.

> Although I do have a thing for big woman. I hope me asking you to dinner doesn't give you any impression that you are more attractive than you think you are. You just seem like an easy target with potential low self-esteem. I also know fat chicks give good blow jobs and are easy to push to the curb when you're done with them. A plump chick with high self-esteem is like a unicorn out here. It's kinda refreshing and sad at the same time. You must be very lonely and you must cry often . . . You should be happy people are asking you out at all still, seeing in five years with that dumpy ass no one will give a shit. Best of luck, hope I didn't give you the wrong impression that you were hot just because I asked you to dinner, PIG.

You got that ladies? Don't go thinking you're hot shit because you're not, and that's the reason this guy wants to fuck you, because he feels sorry for you and you would be desperate for it, because you're a disgusting monster who nobody would want to fuck. The logic is so airtight, it reminds me of a schoolyard fight that two thirteen-year-old girls had during my first week of high school. After a bout of pulling each other's hair and being restrained by their respective friends, one of the girls dealt the final blow by spitting out: 'You're an ugly slut who can't even get any.' Forget the Madonna *or* the whore: #getyouagirlwhocanbeboth

The same weekend Faverman's horrifying tirade was shared online, so was a music video by Joe Jonas's synth-pop band DNCE that went a long way in soothing the wounds. The clip, for the track 'Toothbrush', features Jonas – whose dating history is littered with models and other professionally thin women, including Taylor Swift and Gigi Hadid – chasing plus-size model Ashley Graham around his apartment and the streets of New York City, as the song begs her to leave her toothbrush – the universal symbol for *more than a one-night stand* – at his house. Earlier in 2016, Graham became the first ever plus-size woman to appear on the cover of *Sports Illustrated's* Swimsuit Issue, an annual honour usually reserved for models with the tiniest waists and biggest tits. But despite being a landmark moment for plus-size visibility, compared with the 'Toothbrush' clip, that cover barely registered on my groundbreaking barometer.

I wasn't expecting to feel so emotional over a video for a song by a band featuring a former Jonas Brother, but that was until I saw the shot of Graham dropping Jonas's hand and cheekily running away from him on the street. She is carefree and playful – two things fat women are rarely allowed to be on screen without being pigeonholed as the jolly fat girl or, in the simplistic words of Gervais's character, the 'happy, bubbly ones'. This simple gesture speaks volumes and it felt momentous. Normally, love feels like a prize that fat girls aren't in the running for. We don't fulfil the criteria. The messages I've absorbed from the world are to be available at all times and to sacrifice my self-worth if it means I won't be alone; to say yes to anyone at all, because you never know when (or if) you'll be asked again. More than anything, though, we are reminded to take what we can get, and never to even think about playing hard to get.

The last time I tried – really tried – to date someone, it felt like a sure thing. He knew and respected my work, had sought me out at parties and events and sent all the right signals that he was interested. I pursued it and we spent a lot of time together, before I learned he'd had a girlfriend all along. 'For once I thought I didn't have to worry that seeing me/my body would be a dealbreaker,' I wrote in my journal, burned by the lasting effects of online dating culture that tells you your pictures should make you look good, but that good = thin, and that making yourself look thin is a lie when you're not, and if anyone thinks you *do* look good in your photos, they'll be horrified to see the reality. 'The more times this happens, the harder it becomes to imagine any alternative,' I wrote. 'This time I thought it would be different, but of course it wasn't.'

That DNCE video gave me hope, though, because when Graham runs away, the tag on her clothes might show a double-digit number, but Jonas still follows. He wants her to come back and he wants her to stay. This brief moment felt full of potential and hope. He desires her in a way that isn't fetishistic or disposable; it's neither because or in spite of her body. He likes her for her, in the most Bridget Jones, Blessid Union of Souls kind of way. I know he can't be the only one who feels like that.

CHAPTER 12

HELD BACK BY THE LOVE THAT WOULD NOT GIVE THEM UP

David Bowie died today, and I hope by the time you read this I feel better than I do right now. It's eight months before I have to submit this book to the publishers, then it'll be many more months until anyone will be able to buy it. I'm sure I will cry over a lot of different things between my now and your now, but right now in this now it's been only a few hours. We're in the middle of a heatwave so it's too hot to dance and too hard to not cry. All I can think about is how sad the world feels, and how I know that because of the cumulative mourning pouring into my Twitter, Instagram and Facebook feeds.

I search my phone to find a photo of my friend Minna and I standing under the neon sign declaring DAVID BOWIE IS YOURS at last year's *David Bowie Is* . . . exhibition opening at ACMI in Melbourne. It's the only photo I have from that night, aside from one of me laughing while holding two tiny ice-cream cones. I crop the photo in Instagram, apply a filter, draft a caption that's loaded with the required emotional weight today calls for – something like *yours, mine, ours, always* – then cringe at the nakedness of my feelings I'd dare to share, close the app, open it again and keep scrolling.

The truth is, my own relationship to Bowie's life and music and legacy is more about my mother than the singer. In my early twenties, my trips back home were opportunities for me to riffle through the record collection she cultivated in her teens and twenties, a time when she loved Bowie's music. I'd pilfer the albums I loved (or the ones I thought might make me seem cool if someone else saw them on my shelf), wrap them protectively in jumpers and place them between shoes and toiletries in my suitcase. Listening to *Aladdin Sane* means listening to the same grains on the vinyl disc my mum did when she was sixteen. It means seeing her name and childhood address scrawled in her familiar looping cursive script on both sides of the record. She stamped out a label with her name in protective block letters and stuck it above Bowie's left ear on the iconic album artwork. To the right of his lightning-painted face she wrote her two best friends' names below the 'logo' she drew on all her favourite albums: her name, Dawn, inside a rising sun. Listening to the record again, knowing that Bowie is gone, makes me hold tight to this physical memory of my mum's love of his work. I can imagine the way her knees and hips bent and twisted when she heard 'Jean Genie', a movement that embarrassed me as a kid and I adore now.

I hold inside, in equal measure, sadness that he is gone, and relief that she isn't, that the cancer that took him away didn't beat her either time it invaded her body. I do what we all do when we hear news of a famous artist dying: I make it about myself.

Someone on Tumblr shares a screenshot of a tweet that Gerard Way, the singer from My Chemical Romance, wrote almost two years ago, about dead artists returning to the cosmic dust and becoming part of the place where ideas come from. It felt right for today, the original poster explains, and reminds them of Bowie. It's a moving but unrelated nugget of romanticism, infused with the hope we need to be reminded of today. The internet is flooded with people tying this very tangible and permanent loss to their ephemeral and innately personal feelings about Bowie's music and style and legacy. Each of these posts feels like we're screaming, *I AM FEELING THIS TOO. THIS MATTERS TO ME AS WELL. I AM HURT AND I CARE.*

My best friend's grandmother died a few weeks ago. I never know what to say when someone is grieving or hurting – my go-to reaction, in my own mind, is generally that of Liz Lemon from *30 Rock* patting her sobbing boyfriend on the back and murmuring, 'It okay. Don't be cry.' I offered to drive my friend to the beach, and later researched the name of her grandma's favourite type of flower; she recognised them while we were going for a walk but didn't know what they were called. They were hydrangeas, and a big bush of them outside my front door is currently suffering in the January heat. When my friend's mum posted a photo of her late mother on Facebook, I liked it to show that I knew and understood and cared, a move that felt at once like the most and very least I could do.

This is how we mourn now, or at least it's how we share our loss with the world. It's also how we offer support and comfort. It never feels quite enough to use the internet to communicate grief – one of the most private and personal things besides maybe sex and whispering – but at the same time its inherent public-ness means that it feels like so much. Depending on the level of your privacy settings, literally anyone in the world – anyone you went to primary school with, anyone you worked a part-time job with, anyone you met at a party – could be invited to access your grief. There's not a lot of difference between mourning the loss of a friend or celebrity with an Instagram post than there is announcing the birth of a child or an engagement or any other non-breeder life event in the same way. I need to remind myself of that every time I feel my hackles rise when the person in the memorialised photo is somebody I care about.

It's been almost two years since my friend Marcus died, but his Facebook page is still full of sweet words from people whose minds are sprinkled with memories of him. That page on the internet has become like a gravestone, but the flowers on it never wilt. They're just replaced with fresher posts, or ones that Facebook's algorithm decide are in bloom that day. The 'I barely knew you, RIP' comments that proliferated in the days and weeks after news spread of his death have been phased out now. I hated those messages. I hated seeing the thumbnail-sized faces of people who knew him – or talked openly about how they didn't – and being privy to their memories of him. More than that though, I resented the people for whom public grieving came so easily, when I could barely articulate the ache in my heart that made it hard to get out of bed, or the guilt I felt at not doing more for him when I knew he needed someone to be there. The guilt was only ever replaced by a total helplessness and inability to think of what – if anything – could have let us keep him.

But I had no right to feel as angry as I did. Those sentiments weren't contributing anything to my mourning, but it's not like they were taking anything away from it either. In an episode that touched on the repetitive online memorials that proliferated around the 2015 terrorist attacks on Paris, the co-host of the podcast *Reply All*, PJ Vogt, offhandedly commented on the trend wherein thousands (or millions) of people chime in on a tragedy that doesn't directly affect them. 'To me, that's like, one of the nice things about the internet: people feel things and want to express them.' This perspective was an optimistic look at the more cynical backlash against the seemingly empty digital responses to the attack. The conversation on the podcast moved on quickly, but I stayed right there. This episode of *Reply All* came out almost a year to the day since Marcus died, and it would be a few months before the planet shook for a moment as news of Bowie's death spread across it. And I realised what a dick I was being. I love having feelings on the internet; you wouldn't be reading this book if I didn't have so many of them, so loudly, so openly.

I genuinely admire people who can make themselves so vulnerable, the ones who don't need to work hard at chipping away at their protective shields – or who haven't constructed them in the first place – like the ones I've built up so I don't have to open myself up. But being that honest, laying yourself bare like that is scary as shit. And I was mad that other people could be so open, so public, so transparent in their pain while I tried to push mine down and pretend it didn't hurt. It would've been simple to do the bare minimum and share the photo of Marcus and me, taken at a time when we straddled the puberty equator from opposite ends – me, fully grown at thirteen; him, weedy at twelve, with a mouth full of braces – but I escaped that public performativity and instead took out my journal for the first time in more than a year, and tried to remember every detail about the afternoon we spent together when he was fourteen and supposed to be teaching me to play a Dashboard Confessional song on the drums, but instead we lay side by side on the floor of his practice room, talking about scary real shit like school and our parents and moving away, while we sipped warm Cokes and let the scratchy fibres of the Afghan rug tickle the backs of our shoulders.

Describing someone you're close with as being 'like the brother you never had' is such a cliché, but there's no other phrase that does justice to how I felt about Marcus. I stuck up for him at school when he had those braces and curls covering his eyes, and he told me he was proud of me when he'd outgrown me by a foot and we only saw each other on my annual trip back to our hometown each Christmas.

After weeks of drafting notes and deleting them, of trying to watch the videos he'd recorded of his travels and adventures but being unable to hear his voice for more than a few seconds, of bitterly scrolling through the swarm of posts recounting shared experiences with this very special boy, I just visited his Facebook page and pasted a link to a song called 'It's Alright, I Understand' from an album that came out a few days before he died, by The Smith Street Band, who we'd talked about in our last conversation together.

I don't think I'll ever quieten the desperate voice in my head that wonders if Marcus had spent any time listening to these songs about battling depression, or if his eyes stilled over the track called 'I Don't Want to Die Anymore', like mine did when

I scanned the liner notes in the days and weeks after his mum told me that we'd lost him.

Writing anything else made me feel like I do when I see friends in separate cars recognise and acknowledge one another while I wait at a set of traffic lights: they're familiar to each other, and there's a history or shared joke in their gestures and mimes, but to bystanders like me, there's a dissociation between the friendship I'm observing and the one that really exists. We're just outliers, piecing together a connection from the clues we're allowed to see. We'll never really get the full picture. I didn't want to let anyone else in on the final moment I was sharing with Marcus, safe behind the windshield of my car. I didn't want anyone else to see me feeling in the way I observed them all doing the same thing. I just wanted to play that record over and over and hope that it would somehow be coated with a veneer of my memories of him in the same way the Bowie record is infused with memories of my mum.

It happens every time somebody loses their somebody, and the sentiment is no less significant because it's expressed digitally. Before we had Twitter we might've called each other or written about it or sought out a friend to comfort over a shot of whiskey or five. I get a kind of generational cringe when I realise the time to do those things is passing, and now the best we can hope for is for our sentiments about a famous person to be shared by enough people that they're aggregated into a journalism-lite blog post with a name like '75 Times People Were Sad About [Insert Celebrity Death Here]'.

This is why I stayed quiet when my beloved grandfather died less than a year after Marcus did; because my feelings for a man so beloved that the word 'beloved' didn't even suffice, could not be contained in a post or picture. But I realise now, with hindsight, that saying *nothing* didn't feel right either. It felt like I'd skipped a phase in the mourning process, like I hadn't sufficiently warned the people who encountered me that I was hurting, because I didn't acknowledge it on social media, like a digital 'Keep off the Grass' sign, an invisible black veil, pulled down over my face as a way to signal from a distance that you need to tread carefully.

I already had a tattoo in honour of him, one that I'd gotten four years earlier, and considered expanding it to be a more thorough and obvious memorial that would stay on my skin forever. Maybe I'd post a photo of the completed design on Instagram so everyone knew in that moment – and everyone who met me afterwards and for the rest of my life would know – that a piece was missing. I didn't do that. Instead I propped up a worn paperback book called *His New Nanny* on a tiny display on my desk. Grandpa gave me the Mills and Boon romance novel when I last saw him. I'm looking at it now as I write this. The day he said I could keep it, he was too old and frail to get out of his chair, his mind disappearing and taking with it his ability to read the horny words on those pages, as he'd done with other similarly pulpy novels every day I'd known him. He was long past being able to pull a paperback out of his back pocket and stretch out on the hard floor to read it before a nap; or braid my hair as I sat on his knee; or carve the baked ham perfectly at Christmas; or teach me to waltz, or play tennis; or collect donations for the RSL; or erect a croquet course in his backyard for his grandkids; or carry me on his shoulders like when I was tiny and thought he was the tallest man in the world. He was already on his way then, but he left a piece of himself stapled to the pages of the book, like Tom Riddle did to Ginny Weasley's diary (only less evil), that I'll forever feel when I look at its airbrushed cover illustration of romance novel seduction. Having that book and those memories is enough without any broadcasting taking place.

I woke up in Los Angeles the day Prince died. Anton and I were staying in an Airbnb for a week, before I flew back to Melbourne and he returned to New York. He got up and went for a run in Griffith Park while I cracked open my computer and saw the initial reports from TMZ. I waited for confirmation from Paisley Park before I let myself move beyond that hesitant state of limbo grief. By the time Anton walked in the door, Prince was officially gone. I was so grateful, that day, for the community of voices who could vocalise their sadness more effectively than I could. On MTV's memorial podcast, fittingly titled 'Dearly Beloved', the writer Doreen St Félix said, a mere five minutes after the *Associated Press* confirmed the news, 'Today is April twenty-first. And it snowed in April today.'

That night, my friend Ariel took Anton and me to Smog Cutter, a bar in Silver Lake, to do karaoke. We arrived and bought a round of beers just as a woman was going HAM on the microphone singing a Mariah Carey song. It took a few minutes for the host to realise the woman was destroying the mic and he'd need to put the karaoke on pause while he repaired the damage. A kid near the pool table desperately cried, 'Who cares?! Prince is dead! Play Prince!' He drunkenly warbled the chorus from 'Purple Rain' to the silent bar a few times before it kicked in for real on the jukebox and drowned out his desperate, drunken memorial.

A few days later, Bruce Springsteen performed in concert dressed in purple instead of his usual black. During the set, he covered 'Purple Rain' in tribute to Prince. Springsteen didn't only understand that people needed to release their sadness into the world instead of trapping it inside – he also knew they needed to do it communally, be that in a stadium or a bar in East LA or on the internet.

No message I wrote could do justice to Marcus or his death or our friendship. Nothing I said could make me feel like I did when he laughed or when he hugged me after we hadn't seen each other in a year. Nothing on the internet could represent what this very real and tangible and not at all digital loss felt like, or make it any better. But we don't post about sadness on the internet to heal. It's not to make it better or pretend it didn't happen; it's a way of saying *I felt this too; this person's life mattered to me, and their death does too.* It's about creating a communal sensation of mourning and understanding.

The day after Prince died we took a drive out to Culver City with my friend Marie to visit the Museum of Jurassic Technology. A place whose intentions are as mysterious as the objects within its walls, the museum is difficult to understand and at the centre of many feuding theories. Some suggest that a few of its strange collections are rooted in truth and it's up to the viewer to decide which elements are false; others say it's a testament to since-debunked theories and ideas – things we thought before we knew better. For all its focus on memory and creation and magnetics, the museum feels preoccupied with death. Its barely lit rooms can feel claustrophobic, and reading the didactic panels pinned to the walls can often feel like you're observing an epitaph attached to a tombstone.

One collection eulogising long-dead ideas is filled with anecdotal remedies and superstitions – or what it calls 'vulgar knowledge' – about all matter of subjects, and each description is accompanied by a crudely simplistic model figurine. The room is called 'Tell The Bees: Belief, Knowledge & Hypersymbolic Cognition', and references the ancient act of informing a colony of bees when a family member dies, otherwise the bees will follow suit. This elaborate and bizarre ritual, which also involves inviting the bees to attend the funeral and bringing them 'funeral sweets', is one of the more thorough and considered practices in the exhibition. Another crude display – which could double as a horror film synopsis – simply says, 'A woman after childbirth is the most dangerous thing on earth. All sorts of uncanny things are around the mother and infant, and if she goes to a river to wash, the fish will go away.' It's spelled out underneath a small model of a bed.

Passing through the collection, I could feel myself soften because time after time I was confronted with expired theories, ideas and traditions about how we mourn the people we love, none of which are any more or less legitimate than the ways that we memorialise one another today. The 'cures' are about fending off death, and the superstitions are about allowing it to occur in the most romantic ways. There's the one about how white moths that fly at twilight are the souls of the dead, who 'are allowed to take farewell of this earth' in that lepidopteran form.

The most stunning of the folkloric rules in the museum is one called 'Crying Back or "Wishing" the Dying', which tells us to leave the side of the person we love to allow them to die peacefully. It's designed in service of the person who is passing:

If a person is withheld from dying by being cried or wished back, the person called back will "die hard" and be deprived of one or more faculties as a punishment to the parent or other relation who would not acquiesce in the Divine will.

But its encouraging resolve is also a gentle motivator to surviving loved ones to let go, no matter how hard it might be. It tells us to 'leave the room' – whether literally or emotionally – lest they be 'held back . . . by the love that will not give them up.' That urgent love is framed as a more painful option than letting go.

This, and all the other fragments of 'vulgar' knowledge are collected in *Guide Leaflet No. 3*, published by the museum's trustees and for sale in the gift shop for a few dollars. It contextualises the sometimes silly, often harrowing theories using penicillin as a case study: if nobody had trusted in Alexander Fleming's fungal broth – *his* vulgar remedy – we'd all have flown away as moths by now. The leaflet's afterword reminds us of this fact, of the wisdom of everyone who's invented and theorised and passed on, by crediting those past for creating a road map to life, in the form of this vulgar knowledge.

In her tribute to Bowie, the singer Lorde wrote on Facebook (where else?) that the way we relate these world-shaking tragedies to ourselves as a type of public and collective grieving feels garish to her, but that ultimately it was essential and in keeping with the way Bowie's work had uniquely impacted everyone who encountered it. The universally personal tone we took in our remembrances was 'almost selfish, like therapy', she wrote, because, to all of us, 'he was a piece of bright pleated silk we could stretch out or fold up small inside ourselves when we needed to.' He was a simulacrum for our deepest fears or hopes or desires, and so it made sense that losing him felt personal, even if we didn't all know him personally.

When it comes to celebrities, we often treat death less like tragedy and more like opportunity; a way to take a piece of what they were and parse it through our experience, in the hope that the world understands who they were specifically to us. Bowie was his own piece of silk but he belonged to the world by letting us all hold a thread. When you take all those threads that you will sorrowfully collect over a lifetime, you'll have enough to weave into a sheet, on which you will have enough room to write down what they all meant to you.

CHAPTER 13

THEY BUILT A STATUE OF US

Tonight I elbowed my way to the front of the crowd. It had been years – at least six or more – since I'd had the nerve and gumption and desire to press my shins against the edge of a low stage in a tiny band room because I couldn't bear the thought of the sound passing through anyone else's ears before arriving in mine. It had been so long since I'd been that close to a band that actually meant anything to me, one that made me unable to pretend to play it cool.

But Girlpool are in town and their songs about walks home and trash cans and getting head while watching movies are so important to me; they make me feel connected to my best friend, Anton, who lives continents away and listens to the same songs at the same time as I do, and to my friend Maquarie who had no idea she introduced me to the band until I told her so as we stood in the courtyard of the venue nervously drinking a Coke (her) and smoking cigarettes (me) before it was time to tear our hearts open and patch them up again with Cleo and Harmony's harmonies. She tweeted, 'My friend Brodie was like let's stand at the stage and I pretended like I wasn't into that but I was'.

I pretended I didn't care that I was too tall to stand so close to the stage because standing there – shifting my weight from one foot to the other, never knowing what to do with my hands (putting them on my hips felt too posed, crossing them over my chest felt too cynical) so I just clasped them in front of my stomach and picked all my fresh nail polish off – made me forget that earlier in the day I'd had an argument with a friend I'd never argued with before. It was one of those conversations that sprouts from misunderstanding but before we knew it we were both defensive and emotional and unable to see from the other person's perspective. It was a fight that was so awful it had me crying those silent, heaving tears at my desk and my back still aching a day later.

Being there helped me forget the deadline that had been looming, large and heavy and foreboding, over my head for weeks. It made me feel like Anton was here with me, not a million miles away, trudging home in the aftermath of Winter Storm Jonas. He'd been as much a teacher to me as he'd been a confidant and collaborator over the eight years we'd known each other. He introduced me to movies, books, artists and film-makers I'd never heard of before but, with his passion and my own research, I grew to love. I grew to love the things he intro-duced me to so fully that sometimes I had tiny crises, where I wondered if I couldn't think for myself; if I could only enjoy something if someone I trust co-signs it; if I didn't actually love these things as much as I loved Anton. Other times I pushed the doubt away and held tight to the bands like Girlpool or the books like Emma Straub's *Modern Lovers* that we discovered and loved independently of each other, but shared when we were reunited over Skype or after long flights.

That's the power of being one ripple in a heaving ocean of fans, all holding a collective breath when we know a note or lyric or chord change is coming, one we've listened to alone in our bedrooms and headphones, that we're now experiencing so publicly and obtrusively. It's an experience that's at once designed just for me and without any thought of me at all. It's what my friend Minna, who went alone to see Madonna perform after decades of obsession with the singer, summed up by writing, 'it seemed appropriate that my fandom culminated in what I hoped would be a sublime experience, alone alongside 15 000 people'. I matter so little in the grand scheme of things, but that bruising in my shins that I'll feel tomorrow serves as a reminder that I made myself matter in the biggest and most personal way tonight.

A year earlier, in March 2015, I woke up to find that my friends in other states and countries had sent me a flurry of text messages from the earliest hours of the day. I instantly knew something was wrong. D'Arcy was the first to text me, at 4.16am, saying, *I'm so afraid you're asleep right now and I don't want to be the one to tell you . . .* I opened Twitter, and saw dozens of people I know, or who knew enough about me to know I'd have a reaction to knowing what happened, asking somebody nearby to check and see if I was okay, saying I was the first person they'd thought of when they'd heard the news.

Nobody had told me the 'news' directly, they all just wanted to sympathise or reach out or let me know I was in their thoughts on the day Zayn Malik left One Direction. Before I even read the announcement, I knew in my heart and my bones and my guts it was something to do with that band. Despite loving and consuming and listening to and talking about so many different aspects of pop culture, it was this boyband I was most vocal about, and so many people associated me with. My first thought was that the band had broken up. The next was that Zayn had died – I don't know why my mind immediately attached itself to his name, but it did.

When I saw the official announcement posted to the band's Facebook page, I cried tears of relief – *at least he's still alive*, I reasoned – before sitting on the edge of my bed, folding in half and crying, half out of sadness and half out of pride that he'd made the decision to do the hardest thing. I bet if anyone had peered into my bedroom that morning, I'd have looked like an elderly widow in a TV movie who's struggling to readjust to sleeping in a big old bed without her husband snoring beside her. Instead I was a 25-year-old woman who felt a bookmark being placed in a very specific and special chapter in her life, knowing the story would continue but not in the same way. Just a 25-year-old woman who had to get dressed and go to work and explain that, yes, I really was crying and, no, it wasn't a joke.

I had to endure a day of sitting on the internet and scrolling past clickbait stories of parents cruelly filming their teenage daughters who were visibly and audibly devastated by the news. I couldn't relate to the adults in those situations, the ones who found their daughters' pain so funny and insignificant when I knew what those girls knew: something that had brought us comfort and companionship and community for five years had splintered and couldn't be pasted back together.

I got a call to do an interview about what Zayn's departure meant for fans, and was called a 'One Direction expert' in the article's headline. I was asked to record an interview for a documentary about boybands and fangirls, as a way to 'mark this important heartbreaking moment'. I left work early and cried off all my make-up, then shakily reapplied it before the director arrived and made a permanent record of me trying to process.

After she packed up her gear and went home, I was left alone for the first time since I'd woken up and heard the news that morning. I checked in on D'Arcy – she was in Los Angeles and I was in Melbourne, but our internal and emotional clocks still synched up somehow. We'd become friends just a few months earlier via an article I wrote about my relationship to One Direction, in which I expressed a mass of feelings about the band and what it meant to love them as an adult, feelings she'd also had. We'd texted almost every day since then, but were still a year away from meeting in person.

Our relationship was one of the gifts One Direction gave me. That, and a feeling of instant understanding with people who, like me, have felt like the oldest and most eager people at enormous stadium concerts, spent late nights watching YouTube clips of British talk shows from 2011, and waited in line to watch a documentary that promises new insight into the lives and minds of five young men we know both everything and nothing about. No matter how hard we tried, we couldn't explain what all of that felt like to anyone who hadn't done the same things and had the same immediate, confusing and visceral reaction. 'Hard day. Sad sad. Bad day,' D'Arcy wrote to me. 'Glad I have you in my life.'

A month before that it was Valentine's Day, and I was at a One Direction concert, staring at Zayn through the tiny lens of my camera, knowing then that it wasn't going to be forever. His downcast face set off a whirring ball of worry inside me, prompting an urgent, Miss Clavel-esque response that *something is not right*. I spent half the show with my eyes glued to the tiny boys on the enormous stage, trying to decipher what they were thinking and feeling with every flip of Harry's hair or whispered personal joke shared between Louis and Liam, and the other half taking in the fever pitch of the teengirlhype that enveloped it.

~~They~~ *We* love these boys and their music with everything ~~they~~ *we* have, but that love is just as much about the cute faces and the choruses as it is about how those things allow us to mine something deep within ourselves and offer it up without shame or fear. Four years earlier I would've been on the side of the disgruntled commuters put out by the tens of thousands of concertgoers swarming on a football stadium at peak hour. I would've been the pompous jerk who assumes that anyone who listens to a boyband is missing the essential part of their brain that filters the musical curds from the whey.

But I wasn't, because I was lucky enough to find One Direction during a time in my life when my critical guard was lowered. And I discovered the whey is fucking dope and essential to the production of cheese!

The band had skipped Australia on their world tour a year earlier, in support of their third (and my favourite) album, *Midnight Memories*, so the intensity of adoration and thirst in the stadium was amplified because we had waited so long to see them, relying only on the videos and photos our fellow fans in the global network of Directioners had ladled out for the past year.

During that period of physical absence I grew to appreciate this fandom for what it was: a living, breathing, heaving ecosystem filled with 'me too!' moments, giving disparate people in every imaginable pocket of the world a way to understand one another. I was there with my main girl Sinead and her mum on one side of me, and my friends Nico and James on the other. I had met James through the Tumblr fandom of adult Directioners, then in person outside one of their shows in Melbourne during the last tour. He and Nico connected in the same digital space, and within a few months they were in love, travelling back and forth between Melbourne and Baltimore, where Nico was living at the time. They stayed as long as their tourist visas would allow, until Nico relocated to Melbourne permanently. I wrote a reference to back up the validity of their relationship as part of Nico's visa application. He made a quick return trip back to the States alone, because he had already bought tickets to see One Direction perform there, on the tour that didn't include Australia. Tonight, in the steaming hot stadium in Melbourne, they were seeing the band together for the first time. Finally, after all the waiting, here the band was before us – the five of them together in front of the five of us, for one of the last occasions – like ideas we'd philosophised over for aeons, dreams come true.

Being in that stadium felt like more than just being among my people, it felt like I was one of a lucky few bearing witness to a solar eclipse: something that was shimmering and glorious for just a moment, before it disappeared again for god knows how long. When I think about One Direction fans, I think about how that stadium felt, pulsating with the energy of people who were experts in their field coming face to face with the subjects they'd spent years studying; when I think of the way the (mostly, but not entirely) young girls in that stadium clutched at themselves and one another during Zayn's high notes or Harry's jokes or the moment in the song 'Better Than Words' when Niall grabs his crotch, I see them as gobsmacked astrologers viewing a supermoon for the first time in decades: *here it is — the thing we've dreamed of and read about and hoped for — right in front of us.*

Despite the fact that a month later everything would be different, in that moment we all felt so lucky.

Stepping foot inside Graceland felt like the culmination of a lifetime's worth of love. I couldn't name more than one or two of Elvis Presley's songs as a little kid, but that didn't stop me from obsessing over him. I hung a poster of his face above my single bed with fairy sheets; I asked for a guitar and lessons for my eighth birthday in an attempt to be more like him; I cried hysterically when my mum bought me a Disco Ken doll on a rare trip to a department store out of town, so horrified that she had misunderstood my request for an Elvis collectible wearing a miniature leather suit like the one my idol had worn for his 1968 Comeback Special concert; I collected worn paperback biographies from garage sales and memorised their contents with the kind of dedication I can't imagine that, with the existence of Wikipedia, I could replicate today. And I wasn't the only one. As well as memorialising his life and work, Elvis's beloved home was also a reminder of the timelessness and universality of fandom.

After a long day driving to Memphis from New Orleans, my friends Emily, Nadia and I followed the glimmering signs and pulled our rental car into the packed parking lot. It was 4pm on a grey, gloomy Wednesday and there were hundreds of fans from all over the world who had also come to be in the place where Elvis's legend was cemented. We walked through the front door and saw his custom-made couch in the sitting room, and the bedroom his parents lived in until his mother's death. I saw the tableware he and Priscilla used at their wedding, and the kitchen where his famous heart-bursting peanut butter banana bacon sandwiches were prepared. I saw Lisa-Marie's favourite stuffed toy, and stood in the room where our audio tour guide, John Stamos, told us that Elvis played piano for his friends one last time before retiring to the bathroom and from the world that day in August 1977.

I had never had such intimate access to the private inner world of someone who had contributed so much to mine. It was overwhelming to see fragments of myself scattered among the exhibitions. (If you thought I couldn't turn the home and legacy of someone like Elvis into a story about myself, you underestimated ya girl.) I recognised my adoration in the handmade, fan-made paraphernalia decorating the Trophy Building; I understood the motivation behind the paintings of Elvis propped up against the furniture in his father Vernon's office. The subject of our fandom might flicker and change from person to person, but we're all united in the practice of loving. If I'm in the business of obsessing, then Graceland was my professional summit.

Finally, after weaving in and out of the house, its yard and external rooms filled floor-to-ceiling with platinum records, we came out into the light of the Meditation Garden. I wasn't expecting what I'd find there. For all my reading and memorising almost twenty years earlier, I didn't know Elvis Presley was buried in the gardens of Graceland and that I'd one day find myself holding back tears as I hovered over his gravestone. I'd later learn this wasn't his original resting place – for the first two months after his death he was buried alongside his beloved mother Gladys in the nearby Forest Hill cemetery. His dad then brought them to Graceland to rest alongside Elvis's twin brother, Jesse, who had died at birth 42 years earlier. It might be easy to view the garden as the end of Elvis's story, but that idea is disproven before it even has a chance to germinate, purely because of the legend-making adoration we've just witnessed inside.

The handcrafted trophies, posters, costumes and detailed oil paintings made by fans that Graceland honours so lovingly all speak to something so much bigger than the enormous mythology of Elvis Presley; they legitimise and value the largely scorned act of fanning, of being in love with the work and idea of a celebrity or pop culture product. Graceland is as much a shrine to the people who loved Elvis as it is to him.

A few weeks after that trip, I visited Seattle to deliver a talk on the interactive nature of One Direction's fans, how effectively we've inserted ourselves into the band's mythology and music, at the EMP Pop Conference (an annual event that critic Jessica Hopper refers to as 'music writer summer camp'). At the time of giving the talk and writing this chapter, One Direction is on a self-imposed hiatus – the band's first ever break from the seemingly endless cycles of recording and touring that we took for granted for over five years – and we don't know if or when they'll return. I closed that paper by explaining that I have no idea what One Direction's return will look like, but I know for sure that the inevitable end of this band will not be on their terms, because the fans literally won't stop consuming them even when there's nothing left to consume. The band may have given us the tools, but we drew up the plans and built the headquarters ourselves. Now it's all ours. The band is the reason for the fandom and the catalyst for the connection, but what we do with it is wholly our own.

CHAPTER 14

THE CODES TO SELF-ESTEEM

My friend Pork Chop asked me recently if I love Justin Bieber's music because I love him as a person, and I said no. Mostly because I'm not really interested in who Justin Bieber is as a person. But then he asked the same question of Kanye West, and the answer became more complicated, because my affection for the rapper goes beyond just enjoying the work he makes. I don't like Kanye's music any more or less because of his personality, but I have an understanding of his music that runs parallel to the bone-deep love I have for him as a human. Kanye's work is endlessly fascinating, and so, consequently, is he, because one cannot exist without the other. He demands total awareness of his life to fully appreciate his work, and vice versa.

Despite having read and written thousands of words about Kanye since my obsession with him began at the same time as my writing career did, I still find it hard to put my finger on why his performance of the song 'New Slaves' on *Saturday Night Live*, when he stared down the barrel of the camera, daring the audience to look away or stop listening, made me sit up straighter and devote so much of my time and energy soaking up, like a thirsty li'l sponge, everything he had to spray at me.

Before that 2013 performance, I was a casual observer. I danced to 'Gold Digger' if someone played it at a party; and *Watch the Throne*, Kanye's 2011 album collaboration with Jay Z, was the soundtrack to the first month I lived in New York – a key era in my life – but I was ultimately more interested in the people he partnered with; people like Spike Jonze, who directed his short film *We Were Once a Fairytale*, and Nicki Minaj, who destroyed all her male counterparts on Kanye's track 'Monster'.

During the early days of Web 2.0 – back when we still called it 'Web 2.0' – the backlash against blogging was focused on the idea that young people were sharing their thoughts with the world and anyone could read them and once they're out there you can't get them back. While ultimately I think that young people who live online are far more aware and careful and savvy than older generations who can't decide what level of trust to grant the internet and wind up tweeting their credit card details and printing emails while complaining about millennials being over-sharers, I have been kept awake at night thinking of work I wrote on the internet that doesn't represent the way I think or feel anymore. A lot of it was about Kanye West. Back when I was an editorial intern at, then the editor of, a culture website, I wrote about Kanye anytime he performed on TV or released a video or did anything mildly newsworthy – because he is news – and in those articles I mimicked the common eye-rolling reading of Kanye West: that he was egomaniacal, too loud, too brash, too much of everything bad. It took him staring into my eyes through a camera and a screen for me to see how much his work relied on his accepting all of those things he had been accused of.

'New Slaves' is a song about being wealthy, famous, successful and black in America. It's about how those first three descriptors don't counteract the fourth. It's about how consumer culture and the still-prevalent fog of racism that America was built on permeates Kanye's life as a newsworthy figure. It's about the prison industrial complex and how Kanye faces the threat of both racial profiling or violence, and the paparazzi in his daily life. After almost three straight minutes of staring down the barrel of the *Saturday Night Live* camera, with a projected image of his eyes blown up to a massive size serving as the backdrop, Kanye spits a challenge to question him, in the final line of the song, as the lights cut out in Studio 8H and he's left alone, only his head and shoulders illuminated. This performance made me finally understand what Kanye had been saying for all these years, and realise that, as a non-famous white woman, I'll never be able to truly understand what he is really saying. It was an essential turning point for appreciating not just the work he makes, but who he is. Because the two cannot be mutually exclusive.

The traits I admire so much in Kanye are the same ones I'm too unsure to embody myself. I wish the confidence he has in his convictions was contagious enough to replace the nervousness and regret that plague my decisions. When someone tells me they enjoy my work, instead of doing as Kanye does (thanking them, and complimenting them on their good taste), I grapple with the overlapping effects of impostor syndrome and self-doubt that convince me the praise isn't mine to hold. I allow fear to restrict and bind me, and I use it as an excuse with the same regularity with which Kanye identifies fear's resurgence and challenges it. Only, he comes out on top.

In the last few years, I have accidentally become comfortable being on stage. Maybe 'comfortable' is the wrong word . . . it's more like, each time I have to stand in front of people and open my mouth to say words that make sense, I feel a little less like I'm going to spew into my lap. But no number of Q&A-style panels or pre-written speeches prepared me for the nerves I felt stepping onto the stage of the Upright Citizens Brigade Theatre in Los Angeles.

I was there for ASSSSCAT, the legendary Sunday night show that began at UCB's first New York venue when 'the UCB four' – Amy Poehler, Matt Besser, Ian Roberts and Matt Walsh – moved there from Chicago and opened their doors to other improvisers, as well as students who wanted to learn from them. ASSSSCAT operates around what's called a 'Harold': a long-form improvised sketch inspired by a single concept, thread or idea. The inspiration comes from a story told by a guest monologist, who, in turn, is prompted by a one-word suggestion shouted out by an audience member. I knew all of this because of the years I'd spent obsessively studying the history and legacy of UCB and *SNL* and Del Close, the infamous improv teacher who inspired so much of what both of those comedy institutions have become. I had been a fan, but when I stepped onto that stage, I was the guest monologist. And I was packing it.

I had made measly and mostly unsuccessful attempts at performing in plays and musicals when I was in high school, but at UCB I didn't have the chance to rehearse any lines or sing or do any accents – aside from my own blend of classic Australian from Queensland, by way of Melbourne's British-tinged version, with a side of 'one year spent in New York City', which had proved enough of a confusing novelty for the Uber drivers of Los Angeles already. I just had to tell four stories, filled with details, that would form the basis of a show I'd been obsessed with from afar for years, performed by a group of improvisers I loved, as one of the theatre's founders ran back and forth across the stage behind me and occasionally tapped me on the shoulder as a prompt to speak again, just as I'd seen him do on the ASSSSCAT DVD I 'accidentally forgot to return' to the video store when I was nineteen.

No pressure, no pressure. I'd only been in the audience for an ASSSSCAT show in New York recently where Kathleen Turner had been the monologist. Now I'd be doing the same job. No pressure at all. Before I walked onstage with the improvisers who'd be making comedy out of my stories, I sat in the green room sipping a beer, willing the two beta-blockers I'd taken before arriving to kick in, trying to make distracted small talk while silently reminding myself of two things. The first was what our friend Nicko had told Sinead and me years earlier, before our first-ever nerve-riddled DJ set: *Excitement and fear are the same chemical. Nerves and adrenalin come from the same place, so just pretend what you're feeling is the good kind of chemical!*

The second was: *Kanye would be scared, but he'd do it anyway.*

They were essential reminders because, of all the feelings that have held on to me, fear has been the one that refused to let go. It's controlled my actions and decisions since I can remember. Before I hit my teens, I began indulging in a regular

NO WAY! OKAY, FINE.

internal loop of fear and hesitation that I know now is called Catastrophic Thinking, a type of anxious behaviour where the worst-case 'what if' scenarios are the ones my mind clings to. If I burned myself sitting around a campfire or hit my head on the bottom of a pool or fractured my wrist riding my bike or got sick after eating risotto I would systematically cross those things off the list of acceptable activities (or meals) for the rest of my life. The possibility of being hurt became instantly too great to risk trying again. I can recognise these regularly occurring bouts of Catastrophic Thinking when they reappear now, but am often still too terrified to take control of them. Professionally, I'm usually vacillating between three unhelpful zones: the fear of dying without making anything that will exist long after I've expired; the fear of being rejected if I dare to make myself vulnerable; and the fear of taking risks but ultimately failing.

Like Paris Geller on *Gilmore Girls* declaring her desire to live her life in a way that will inspire an in-depth biography of herself, I channelled all my silent ambition into my diary when I was 25 and wrote 'I am so terrified of being forgotten, of working so hard and making nothing of value!' It was one of the most honest and earnest things I had ever admitted since the time, four years earlier, when I drunkenly confessed that the end of *The Oprah Winfrey Show* took with it my unspoken life goal of being somehow accomplished enough to one day be inter- viewed on Oprah's couch. I might have been scared to try, not yet encouraged by what Kanye showed fear could do, but I was still hopeful somewhere in the root of my system.

No matter how positive his self-motivated praise is, Kanye is still serving a sentence for what he did the night of the 2009 VMAs. Soaked in alcohol and feeling outrage about what he felt was a disingenuous award process, Kanye chose a form of protest that involved launching himself onto the stage, snatching the microphone from a then-relatively unknown Taylor Swift, and making his feelings known. It was the 'I'ma let you finish' heard 'round the world. In that moment, it all came tumbling down around him; everything he had fought so long to earn was gone in an instant. He was no longer an obnoxious but endearing egomaniac who made great songs; he was public enemy #1. His upcoming tour with Lady Gaga was cancelled, and on the advice of his early supporter Mos Def, he went underground. He hid away in Paris and Hawaii for more than a year while the world began rallying against the very idea of him – a hobby that endures today. People who had previously no idea who the Chicago rapper was would immediately declare him an outrageous and unwelcome presence, and demand to know who he thinks he is going around saying inciteful (and true) things like, 'George Bush doesn't care about black people,' or 'Beyoncé had one of the best videos of all time.' Years later he is still evading the shadow of that night at the VMAs, and his decision to speak truth to power and call out the awards show industry's tendency to overlook the extraordinary achievements of his fellow black entertainers for more palatable and acceptable figures, like Swift. But then, he was painted as just a bully. He was out of control, he was delusional, they shouted. He was also right – a fact that's plain to see today, with the benefit of hindsight – but that didn't matter in the broader narrative then.

Kanye is a hero in the Greek sense of the word. There's a reason that *Hamilton* playwright Lin-Manuel Miranda, when he met Kanye backstage during a performance, told the rapper that the record-breaking musical is all about him. Both men – Alexander Hamilton and Kanye West – used their skills as writers and fighters to create the lives and legacies they dreamed of, and both men's lives were/are marred by heartbreak, setbacks and death. Like the founding father, Kanye is the protagonist in the tragedy of his own life.

In October 2002, Kanye lost control of his rented Lexus and crashed into another vehicle while driving late one night in Los Angeles. Before the accident, he was Roc-A-Fella's up-and-coming new producer, but was struggling to be recognised and respected as the rapper he dreamed of being. He'd been told to stay in his lane, to keep making the type of music that labels and other rappers already liked and wanted from him, instead of the work he really wanted to make. After the accident, he was allowed a break from producing and could focus all his energies on writing for himself. This accident was an essential building block in delivering Kanye West to the world.

Before that night at the VMAs, Kanye thought he already knew what it meant to lose everything he'd earned and everyone he loved, so any act of self-destructive behaviour couldn't hurt him more than he was already hurting. His beloved mother, Donda, had died less than two years earlier, and his engagement with designer Alexis Phifer had ended soon after.

Aristotle suggested the hero becomes tragic when he unfairly receives misfortune, or when it comes to him through errors of judgement or the act of committing wrongs. Kanye's tragic journey has certainly been signposted by acts for which he's responsible – like the VMAs and the car accident – as well as those outside his control (the death of his mother, the prevalent media narrative of him as an arrogant black man whose opinions are wrong and unwelcome). Perhaps the greatest misconception about Kanye is that his braggadocio makes him automatically out of touch, or that his self-confidence is untoward or unearned – the subtext being that he should mumble his achievements, and sing or talk about anything apart from himself or else he'll forever be branded as arrogant. His songs are laced with details about his history, his come-up, and the obstacles that appeared along the way. Like Alexander Hamilton (who, I should mention, exists in this context as the character Lin-Manuel Miranda created, not the actual Treasury Secretary whose face graces the American ten-dollar bill), Kanye needs to be the author of his narrative, because he knows his circumstances and story better than anyone else, and besides – if he didn't do it, who would? He needs to write his own origin story. He needs to be both Spider-Man and Stan Lee.

Behind this so-called arrogance, the second item on the list of Universally Agreed Upon Things We Should All Hate Kanye For is his supposed lack of self-awareness. After all, we wouldn't have to listen to every commentator's take on his 'ranting' anytime he opened his mouth if he had any self-awareness of his own, right? Not quite. In his 2008 book, *Thank You and You're Welcome*, created in collaboration with graphic designer/ modern philosopher/human quote machine J Sakiya Sandifer, he wrote about his persona, and how arrogance is viewed as his primary flaw. 'If arrogance means being conceited, brash, cocky, or pushy, I can be all of that sometimes,' he wrote, breaking down the fourth wall between himself and the people who talk about him. After writing this passage – that appears as though he's agreeing with his detractors – Kanye shows us the lack of shame that can come with his so-called arrogance, and shows the process naysayers take to arrive at their conclusion: 'I feel my confidence + someone's low self-esteem = my arrogance.'

The root of so much of the finger-wagging and head-shaking cast in Kanye's direction is the result of people's inability to see themselves in him. They view him as an extreme: an extreme version of a celebrity, an extreme version of a swaggering rapper, an extreme version of an Angry Black Man. The strength I take from Kanye's words and his work derives from the ways I am able to see myself in him. I was not brought up by an academic mother who raised me to believe I'd be the Martin Luther King of my generation and a photojournalist father who was once a Black Panther. I am a white woman in Australia with no reference points for his lived experience. But I do know what it feels like to overcompensate with faux-confidence to counterbalance my default setting of insecurity, and hope that talking about myself disguises the reality of my vulnerabilities. I do know what it feels like to raise my hackles and snarl my teeth when I'm asked to explain my words or actions, because I assume every question is an interrogation that requires me to square my shoulders and go on the defensive. Kanye's work is not about me or designed for my comfort or pleasure, I know that, but the humanity of his emotion is universal enough for me to understand and relate to it.

I can recognise the 'how dare you!'s levelled at Kanye when he asserts his right to respect, or positions himself as someone whose voice is worth listening to, because they are the same ones that bounce off the walls of my mind when I speak up or write anything. The act of writing this entire book has been a test of turning down the volume on those voices that question the value and worth of my words. I will never see myself reflected in Kanye's work or experience, but I don't need to; his endurance and resilience and defiance have given me the tools I need to make my own.

A year after the VMAs, Kanye came back. In an interview on the radio station KDWB 101.3, he drew a line in the sand between the comparatively cautious artist he had been in the past and the risk-taker he was now prepared to become. 'I completely lost everything,' he began, referring to the respect, the invitations, the access to worlds he'd battled so hard to be granted space in before that night. 'But I gained everything, because I lost the fear. I used to pray to God to deliver me from pain and fear. And in a way, he did.' The difference between what Kanye lost after that night at the VMAs and what he gained has never been more clear than it is today, when we can see the effects of that shift in his thinking and his strides towards complete creative fearlessness.

'Losing the fear' gave Kanye the freedom to experiment and go big. He made his comeback album, *My Beautiful Dark Twisted Fantasy*, which was accompanied by the grand and exquisite 'Power' film clip and the expansive 'Runaway' short film. He projected his face in an intimately threatening close-up against walls of buildings all over the world to tease the release of *Yeezus*, and sold out Madison Square Garden for a revolutionary and accessible intersection of music and fashion that I watched, live, from a seat in a cinema on the other side of the world. He built a screen, projected onto it an image of the heavens and toured it around the world, with his own personal Jesus in tow, on the Yeezus tour. In 2016, he forced audiences and critics to change the way they viewed and consumed the concept of 'an album' by releasing (then re-releasing, then re-re-releasing) *The Life of*

Pablo as a dynamic and ever-changing record. He made shoes and stores and a family.

By now, he has learned the hard way that saying anything critical about the system in which you operate means potentially losing the access code to that system. But the risk has been minimised since he found that it took losing everything for him to be able to say anything at all. He got the girl and became a father twice over, and all of a sudden his only regret in life became knowing that his mother would never meet his daughter, North West. (His son, Saint, wasn't born when he made this confession.) He crafted a wedding that was as romantic and intimate as it was a piece of elaborate performance art that we could all consume. He broke down the walls that the historically exclusive and exclusionary fashion world had built to keep people like him out. And he did it all on his own terms.

This is why Kanye has become such a significant motivating factor in my life. He has proved, by example, the benefit of fully committing and not even acknowledging hesitation or half-arsery as options. He is a living example of the value of vulnerability and the intrinsic confidence required to pursue a goal you're taught to believe is impossible or unachievable. I sound like I'm preaching, and maybe I am, because another thing I've learned from Kanye is to anticipate a negative response to your ideas and be ready to jump to an emotional defence. (It's how I've ruined a handful of pleasant business meetings: by advocating on his behalf to people I assume don't know him as well as I think I do.)

Kanye is surrounded on all sides by people telling him that his feelings are wrong or invalid or misplaced when he dares to communicate them aloud. He's been talked down to and told that he's too much or too loud. But advocating for respect and inclusion and artistry in the context of celebrity culture, as he's done for more than a decade, is reason enough to listen to what he has to say. Feeling loudly and aggressively and confidently is admirable and enviable.

I was closed off from allowing myself to have clear and visible feelings for the first two decades of my life. I identified early on that my role in relationships was the sidekick, the platonic female cast member in an all-male production, or the friend who was relied on selectively when other options were unavailable. I was the comic relief or the stand-in, never the lead. I knew this, I felt it, I wrote it down, but I didn't dare say it aloud because that would prove that I cared and caring wasn't cool.

Kanye has taken his hesitation and fear of being 'too much' and snapped it into a million pieces like Lindsay Lohan did with that plastic crown at the end of *Mean Girls*. He has dug a pool, filled it with feelings and spent his career swimming laps in it while we all sit around the edges and watch. After leaving a cinema where we'd seen a horror movie, I was explaining to Pork Chop how satisfying it feels to abandon my self-consciousness and react viscerally to the adrenaline that builds up inside me when a heroine bursts through a door or a villain's face appears in a cloudy window. I used to contain my reactions, afraid to laugh with my belly or gasp too loudly and wind up looking like a stock image of 'lady getting spooked at the movies'. Pork Chop asked me why I thought it had changed, and I told him it was not a conscious decision, but probably a roll-on effect of being more comfortable in myself and less concerned with what other people think of how I look/sound/breathe/move. It sounds tiny, but is not insignificant to become comfortable with having visible and audible emotions when you're surrounded by strangers.

In 2008, heartbroken over his mother's death the previous year, Kanye arrived on the Grammys stage filled with grief and ferocity and feelings too incredible to be contained. He performed a sombre rendition of 'Hey Mama' with minimal theatrics – not dissimilar to his stripped back 2015 performance of the song 'Only One'. (I hope you're googling these and watching along as I mention them. Grab some tissues.) 'Hey Mama' was released on his second studio album, *Late Registration*, and was written for Donda before her death. YouTube is filled with footage of her and Kanye performing the song with and for each other (and, in one instance, for Oprah). After her shock death in late 2007, though, the song's message took on new meaning. It became a tribute, a eulogy, surviving proof of all that she meant to him and all he wanted to do for her.

Kanye's fourth album, *808s & Heartbreak*, was an ode to Donda and a reflection of his life without her. The album is now recognised as a modern classic, a daring, powerful and experimental tome of someone mending a broken heart. At the time of its release, though, the sentimental subject matter and primarily auto-tuned production approach was slammed by critics. Kanye had fought so long to be a rapper, and here he was forgoing rapping for singing (kind of badly), crying, clawing at his fresh wounds, howling at the moon about how hurt he was. This is not what we sign up for when we buy a rap album, especially one made by a guy whose public persona is grounded in all the unwelcome, supposedly out-of-touch noise he makes. After spending so long fighting to earn his place in the Mount Rushmore of rappers and trying to make his mother proud, it took losing her for Kanye to open himself up, to present his feelings to the world, and to build his own mountain.

In 2015, when the world was waiting for Kanye to release the album that would become *The Life of Pablo*, he took to the Hollywood Bowl in Los Angeles to perform *808s & Heartbreak* in full. The art, design and fashion elements of his work had become so much more fully realised in the years since the album's release, but the sentiment remained the same; underneath the theatrics and nostalgia was the same sound of Kanye gurgling and struggling for breath as he's drowning in grief, desperation, doubt and fear. Less than six months later, he invited the world to play along with his grief when, at the end of his staggering preview of both *The Life of Pablo* and his Yeezy season 3 collection at Madison Square Garden, Kanye dropped the trailer for *Only One*, a new video game in which the player, riding on the back of a unicorn, is tasked with taking Donda West to heaven, where she will grow her wings.

'For our pity is awakened by undeserved misfortune, and our fear by that of someone just like ourselves,' Aristotle wrote in *Poetics*. Despite all he's endured, both as Human Being and Celebrity, we do not pity Kanye West, the Tragic Hero, because his misfortunes post-2009 VMAs were not undeserved; he himself was responsible for summoning the wrath of the world for daring to point out that a young white woman represented a symbol of power and preference compared to her black peers. He deserved everything he got for making us all listen to his 'rants' when he should've just acted graciously for being allowed an invitation. 'The change of fortune should be not from bad to good, but, reversely, from good to bad,' Aristotle wrote, as if predicting the fall from grace Kanye survived. But we didn't view him as a classic hero, because we didn't fear following in his tragic footsteps, because we refused to see him as a valued human or a relatable figure.

A key trait any Aristotelian hero must possess is a flaw, not one of his own making, but one that dooms him from the start. For Kanye, that is his race. He was never going to be universally accepted or beloved for being a black man who sang about being a black man and collaborated with other black men to make work consumed by a broad audience of not just black men. He is making work about dynamics of race, power and fame in a world where it's still seen by many as more offensive to be called a racist than it is to be on the receiving end of daily racial microaggressions and the victim of bias or violence.

Kanye's confidence should be protected and encouraged, not vanquished or crushed – because it is not cockiness for its own sake; he's made it clear his bravado is a deliberate response to the criticism that pervades his work, and a necessary weapon in his battle against his critics and his own well-documented insecurities. He might argue that the second verse in 'New Slaves' is the greatest rap verse of all time, but he'll just as readily commend Drake for killing the rap game or give credit to Nicki Minaj for spitting the strongest verse on his own album. As a producer, Kanye samples culture and tweaks songs by Billie Holliday, Chaka Khan, Michael Jackson and Elton John. He understands music and his own place within it, and so when he pays himself a compliment, it is not misplaced or delusional arrogance or self-obsession; it's fact. He needs to yell louder than the people who are telling him he's doomed to fail, or their voices will drown out his own.

Critics love to call Kanye an egomaniac, but there's something so powerful and unusual about believing in the art you've created. When Spike Jonze interviewed him in 2007, Kanye explained simply that he is a fan of greatness, so by default he's a fan of himself. This is an essential and game-changing idea: that believing in and loving yourself and your work with the same generosity you give to other people is acceptable and justifiable. Kanye inspires us to be creative and reminds us that we have something important to say, no matter how we choose to say it. And when I say 'us', I'm including Kanye himself. He needs that reminder to continue speaking his truth to power, no matter the consequences. His work gives voice to people like him, and people without the same platforms. It encourages us to build those megaphones for ourselves and love the sounds that come out of them.

A tragic hero is filled with pride, often so much that it becomes a weakness, rather than something to encourage or celebrate. They do not have evil intent. Their actions are grounded in justice or morality. Ultimately, though, Aristotle's tragic heroes are important but flawed human beings. They make mistakes, they stumble, but because of their hubris and nobility, they suffer more than they deserve to.

In February 2015, Kanye returned to the Grammys stage and performed twice. As well as delivering a subdued rendition of 'FourFiveSeconds' with Rihanna and one of the two surviving Beatles by his side, he performed solo, fittingly, the single 'Only One'. Written as a tribute to the women in his life – namely Donda and North, with a nod to his wife, Kim Kardashian West – the song took on new meaning when he stood on that stage, dressed in the clothes he designed for Adidas, with his wife sitting in the front row. He pleaded to be heard, he prayed, and he spat the song's refrain, a declaration that he won't go, to an industry of people who have probably wished, at some point, that he would. The fear that threatened to ruin him six years earlier was nowhere to be seen. After losing everything, Kanye was able to build his new life, create the family he'd been missing and release brave and tender work. He made possessing power seem possible. Instead of just blindly grasping for the life you'll never quite hold, he proved that rebuilding yourself through vulnerability could work, and made clutching, with a strong and assertive fist, that version of a life, feel possible for everyone watching it unfold.

I was that person blindly grasping, in the years BK (Before Kanye); I was scrambling and frustrated. Finding that entry point to his work played an essential role in my ability to open up and be vulnerable and – as much as it sounds like something you'd see on a motivational poster in a guidance counsellor's office – believe in myself, even if that process can be a little terrifying. Kanye takes the things we all know we should do, and questions them. He defies the bounds of our unspoken agreements and pushes at them, to identify their flaws and weaknesses, to test just how aggressively they can constrain us, or how easily they can be destroyed.

I have not overcome fear by any means; Catastrophic Thinking still controls a lot of my decision-making, like whether or not to take my health insurance information to a music festival (YOU NEVER KNOW WHAT COULD HAPPEN), or how to reply to a Tinder message asking me out for a spontaneous drink (in any spur-of-the-moment situation my stress levels rise, I imagine the potential for something going wrong and, more often than not, I choose to jump into a homebound taxi rather than the unknown). But identifying the spiral and acknowledging the firm and reliable ground under my feet and Kanye's voice in my headphones goes a long way in reassuring me that the worst thing that could happen is unlikely to.

In his self-penned cover story for *Paper* magazine in 2015, Kanye assumed the role of modern philosopher and self-love guru. Rather than never having pain, he wrote, bravery and courage are instead about walking towards pain, knowing it's inevitable, but doing it because of what could be on the other side.

I read this when the issue came out, and then I read it again. Something clicked. Spurred on by Kanye's words (plus three glasses of champagne I'd drunk and a little weed I'd smoked at a party), I did something I'd been avoiding and postponing: I laid all my feelings cards on the table and told someone I'd been falling for how I felt about them. I had tried to hide or avoid my feelings for that particular person for months, but I'd done it more generally, with plenty of other people, forever.

I let myself be vulnerable and, like Kanye advised, braced for pain. I might have done it in a careful way – writing and rewriting and running my admission by a few friends for their opinion before finally hitting 'Send' on the email (because a direct conversation is more terrifying than an email, who do you think I am?!) and then taking deep breaths locked inside a bathroom cubicle – but I did it all the same.

For the first time in a long time, I didn't try to avoid my feelings or feel weighed down by their existence. It was a small, emotional, kinda tipsy personal moment, but it went a long way in bursting the bubble of avoidance I'd been suffocating inside. A few days later, I was in the audience of a Wil Wagner show in Melbourne when, in the middle of a song I'd never heard before (and haven't since), he sang, 'Last night I said I love you, nothing exploded and no one disappeared.' I felt the hairs on my arms stand to attention at the certainty of it.

Love is low-stakes. Feelings matter, but don't hold all the power. We infuse them with importance but can deflate them if we need to. Instead of hurting because my feelings in that email weren't reciprocated in the reply, I began to coach myself into feeling proud for having taken the risk, for not scampering away when I reached the edge but instead diving bravely into the pool where Kanye has been doing laps the whole time. We floated there and didn't drown.

AFTERWORD

YOU CAN TOUCH THIS PAGE

On my arm is a stick-and-poke tattoo that bears the name of this book. It came soon after I heard the phrase uttered by the beaten-down manager of a drag club in the movie *Connie and Carla*, and long before even the idea for this book existed. The words encircle the face of an elephant who is fat and kind and has a good memory. It's like a little mirror; a fleshy, freckled reminder of who I am.

My friend Max gave me the tattoo in the kitchen of my old sharehouse the day I learned I had a coffee addiction because, soon after he wiped off the last smear of ink, blood and ointment and left me alone, I fell asleep for 12 hours, waking up only to vomit and google 'brain tumour symptoms', my catastrophic mind jumping immediately to the absolute worst case scenario. Turns out I just needed to put my shoes on and go to the cafe around the corner to ease the withdrawals. (And also cut the fuck back on all the flat whites.) If I'd been able to look ahead in time I'd have known that, but instead I fell into the fear.

I was scared for a long time of putting my ideas and hopes and feelings on paper, because they are not cast in amber; they change every single day and committing them to a permanent record felt like setting myself up for failure. Imagine if Enid Coleslaw from *Ghost World* did this? By the time she finished writing a chapter, her obsessions and annoyances would have shifted so drastically it would be like looking at embarrassing high school photos in real-time. She'd be deleting as much as she'd be writing.

I'm a different person now than I was when the idea of writing a book was first floated by me, and I'm a different person now than I was when, 18 months later, I decided to do it. I'm different now to the person I was when I finished writing everything you've read up until this point, and by the time you read this I'll have changed again. With each cycle of fear-filled 'No way!'s that are eventually replaced by nervous but accepting 'Okay, fine's, everything shifts.

Our hearts and bodies and instincts aren't concrete and permanent, and I see the change happening around me every day. The women in my life are apologising for less and expecting more; historically silenced voices are getting louder; and, with every passing awards season, Kanye West's past declarations seem more and more prophetic. I have empathy now for people who hurt me before, I've unclenched the fists that held on to grudges, and I understand more about my parents than I could ever have hoped to yesterday. Everything shifts.

But while I know it's okay to hold people accountable for the things they said or did in the past, I also need to come to terms with my own change and growth and learning. I think and feel new things every day, and they will be more amorphous and less permanent than the ones inked on these pages. I can erase the new ideas and scribble over the drafts, and maybe there won't be a final one.

You know how up-and-coming bands spend years poring over the songs that tell the stories of their lives up until that point? And then after they get famous and go on tour where they play those songs zillions of times, suddenly that's what their life is? And the things they used to know and think and believe in are contained in the bubble of that first album because, after that, the topics they can write about are reduced to 'fame' and 'being rich'? With any luck that'll be me, after this version of a first album (except replace 'fame' and 'being rich' with 'sleeping' and 'explaining that my tattoo doesn't really mean anything'). This is the archive up until now. I don't remember all the details exactly, and someone else might recall them differently, but the ones I can recall feel like truth to me.

There is an undercurrent of disbelief and doubt and infantilisation when women are asked in interviews how they handle their jobs, or where they find their confidence. Assuming women have negative caches of ability or self-esteem they're battling against at any given moment is never okay – but still, when I'm the one asking questions, I'm often tempted to ask, for purely my own benefit, 'How do you tell yourself you're allowed to do this?!'

NO WAY! OKAY, FINE.

In the time since launching *Filmme Fatales,* my zine about women in cinema, I've interviewed heroes and peers and young up-and-comers, and all I ever want to do is hold them by the shoulders and beg them to let me in on the secret. I might have come far enough to be speaking to them, but I still need them to tell me how to keep going.

One of the interviews I did soon after I started writing for *Rookie* was with Alison Bechdel, whose graphic novels are daring and intimate, and whose comic strip *Dykes to Watch Out For* introduced the world to what's now known as the Bechdel test, a barometer for measuring women's baseline representation in films that influenced much of my early politics around representation on screen.

'Sometimes, when I'm writing personal pieces for *Rookie,*' I said, 'I have to overcome a nagging voice in my head that's saying, *Oh, who'd want to read about me?* Did you have to get over that voice in order to tell your stories?'

'I have to get over that every morning when I get out of bed!' she told me, with a laugh in her voice on the other end of the phone, half a world away. It was an essential assurance from someone whose inspiring work centres around baring herself and her life for us all to consume. It was implicit permission.

I never felt like someone who'd be interesting enough to write about themselves. But now, every day, I do as Alison does, and tell myself – not to convince, but to remind – that I have something to say that is worth listening to. It is not easy, but muzzling the voice in our collective head that tells women their stories are not important is essntial if we have any hope of leaving a mark. I had to confront that feeling every day to get to the point of you touching this page and reading these words. But here you are. Here we both are.

I'm like a living, breathing rejection of a Spoiler Warning; I would rather know what's coming so I can enjoy the adrenaline and frights with the assurance of safety, than venture into the unknown with no information to hold on to. Be it the Red Wedding in *Game of Thrones* or the epilogue set 19 years after the events of *Harry Potter and the Deathly Hallows*, I flick ahead, scroll past the warnings and feel comforted in knowing the end before I go back to the beginning to digest the full course.

If you're like me, and flicked ahead to this page in the book, the biggest spoiler you'll find here is that I wrote a book. Can you believe it's real? I kinda still can't. But it is! It really happened. And now I get to finish a book by writing about how it came to be, just like how Kanye West closed his first album with 'Last Call', a song about his battle to make it to a place where he could release an appreciated and understood album – something he was scared would never happen.

After I finished university, I started projects that never culminated in the zines or webseries or short films or blogs I imagined them being. Somewhere along the way, the vulnerability involved in inserting effort became too intense and threatening, the learning curves and risks started to become too great, the obstacles too high to climb over. I both wanted desperately to be known for something – to contribute something worthwhile to the world and the musical and artistic communities I'd stumbled into – and to disappear and shirk attention because I didn't feel worthy of it. I relied on other people saying things about me to be able to see myself. I spent years deflecting the results of my work and effort, shooing away any compliments or acts of kindness. It wasn't long before my sense of self melted and collected into a puddle, and I was forced to rely on someone else to freeze me and gently sculpt me into something cool and beautiful and shiny.

But at some random, indistinguishable point – because despite what a semi-chronological memoir broken up into chapters will have you believe, life is more like the alien symbols in the movie *Arrival*: lacking a clearly marked beginning, middle and end, and rather just a series of thoughts, messages, moments and realisations smooshed together all at once – I stopped relying on how other people see me to inform how I see myself. At some point, I decided I can't afford to be scared of showing my legs on a hot day or saying something so honest I'm tempted to immediately turn it into a joke, because I need to reserve that fear for the times when I injure myself or someone suggests going on a rollercoaster or I take a chance on a prawn omelette and realise it's undercooked and need a doctor. I need *that* fear to protect me – the rest doesn't require depleting the stockpile. It's not worth it.

Since I wrote the first chapter of this book on 2 January 2016, the world has changed. I got to sit in a dark cinema as Kate McKinnon licked her big action-movie gun and busted ghosts in slow-motion as a revamped version of the original *Ghostbusters* theme pounded in my ears; I got to watch Ashley Nicole Black break out as the star of *Full Frontal with Samantha Bee*, and advocate for black lives during the Republican National Convention (then again at Donald Trump's presidential inauguration); I got to read Lindy West's book, *Shrill: Notes from a*

Loud Woman, and see myself reflected back from its pages so clearly that I was reduced to tears of recognition because Lindy's experience of growing up in her body was so similar to my own; I got to watch Lizzo perform songs about loving what she sees in the mirror while wearing the kinds of outfits women with bodies like hers/mine/ours are warned against wearing from birth. I'm finding, every day, the visible examples of what I can be – the ones I optimistically searched for as a kid but never found – are a reality now. Everything has shifted.

ACKNOWLEDGEMENTS

I'm never going to make an Oscars acceptance speech, so let me have this moment, okay?

Mum, the reason I can and want to do anything is because you've always told me you are proud of me and I'll do anything to hear it again. Thank you Dad, Karli, Shannon and Grandma, for being so loving and encouraging always. Grandpa, I don't think this would've been your thing – it isn't quite Mills & Boon – but I wish you were here to see it. I miss you.

Thank you Sinead Stubbins, for being my friend, for helping me to put a name to my fears and feelings, and for tugging me back down when I get close to floating away. Thank you for always cracking a tinnie and for hiding behind the deck when we played the full version of 'Pyramids' during that DJ set and everyone hated it.

Anton De Ionno, I can't start listing all the things you've brought into my life or I might never stop. Being your friend has taught me like eighty-five per cent of the things I know. Thank you for being the soulmate I will never see naked, and for introducing me to Oliver who introduced me to One Direction.

Thank you Penny Modra, for teaching me so much when I thought I knew everything, and to my buddies at The Good Copy – Pork Chop, Mere, Max, Frunch, Mel – for all the support and for not telling me to shut up when this book was all I could think/talk/stress about.

Thank you Jessica Hopper, not just for telling me I could do it, but for showing me how it's done.

Sarah Laurens, Nadia Saccardo, Minna Gilligan and D'Arcy Carden, thank you for the good vibes, distractions, perspective and friendship. Thank you Greta Parry, Jim Lawrie and Steve Fitzgerald, my Melbourne family.

Thank you Madeleine Dore, for being my human deadline and such an essential and helpful first reader.

Thanks to Nora Ephron and Sidney Prescott, for teaching me to be tough, and to Kathleen Hanna, Chance the Rapper, Lin-Manuel Miranda and Amy Sherman-Palladino for making the work that pulled me through the toughest days of writing.

And to my best friends in the whole world, Kanye, Kim Kardashian, North and Saint West: I love you, can I please have some Yeezys?

My 'tini family – Lola Pellegrino, Brittany Spanos, Gabby Noone, Anna Fitzpatrick, Estelle Tang and Hazel Cills – for being there through every freakout and exciting second. Thanks to Tavi Gevinson for your friendship and encouragement, and to Amy Rose Spiegel, Lauren Redding and every single heart rocket at *Rookie*. Lena Singer and Danielle Henderson, I cannot thank you enough for listening to and then silencing my worries over kugel and coffee (respectively), and for reminding me I have something to say. So many of the stories in book started as ideas for *Rookie* that, under your guidance, I learned to grab hold of and wrangle into something special.

Thank you to Abbi Jacobson, Emma Straub and Courtney Barnett for making work that's so important to me, and saying such nice things about mine.

To Oni Roberts, thank you for a fifteenth year of support, and for being an important early reader.

Infinite thanks to Bronny, Jessica Luxery and Gabi Gregg, and to Kim Selling for *Fat Bottomed Girls*, Lizzo for the *Coconut Oil* EP, Lindy West for *Shrill* and Nicole Byer for *Loosely Exactly Nicole*.

Thanks to Wil Wagner, for writing music that's been a soundtrack to my life in Melbourne, for letting me include your lyrics in this book, and for saying you were excited to read it at a time when you didn't know I really needed to hear that.

Thank you to Jess Cruickshank, who made me feel okay about books being judged by their covers, and made this book look like something I'd want to pick up and keep forever.

Thanks to the team at Hachette: Louise Sherwin-Stark, Justin Ratcliffe, Fiona Hazard, Louise McClean, Dan Pilkington, Katrina Collett, Isabel Staas, Andrew Cattanach and everyone I've met there who's either told me they were excited by my writing or thanked me for showing them a new side to Kanye West (my literal life's work). My sweet publicist Jess Skipper, thoughtful project editor Sophie Mayfield, and my publisher and cheerleader, Robert Watkins, without whom this book literally couldn't have existed; you wanted me to write this when I didn't even know I had it in me.

Thank you to the people and cafes that gave me a place to write, kept me fed and caffeinated and didn't get annoyed when I sat and wrote this book for hours at a time: Everyday Coffee (Collingwood), the Driskill Hotel (Austin), Wild Detectives (Dallas), the Amtrak from Austin to Dallas, The Ace Hotel (New Orleans), Cafe Madeline (Ditmas Park), The New York Public Library (Manhattan), the Amtrak from Portland to Seattle, Mustard Seed Cafe (Los Feliz), Magic Mountain Saloon (Melbourne) and the State Library of Victoria (Melbourne).

Brodie Lancaster is a writer, editor and occasional DJ based in Melbourne, Australia. Her writing has appeared in *Rookie*, *Pitchfork*, *Rolling Stone*, *Jezebel*, *Vulture*, *Hello Mr*, *The Walkley Magazine*, *Junkee*, *Noisey* and *The Pitchfork Review*. She has spoken at TEDxYouth, Melbourne Writers Festival, Emerging Writers' Festival, National Young Writers' Festival and the EMP Pop Conference. *No Way! Okay, Fine.* was shortlisted for The Richell Prize for Emerging Writers 2015 and is her first book.

THE RICHELL PRIZE

The Richell Prize was established in 2014 to assist emerging unpublished writers who are looking to take the next step in their career. Offered annually, it invites writers to submit three chapters of a new work in progress. The winner will receive prize money to support their writing as well as a mentorship with a publisher at Hachette. The goal of The Richell Prize is to help new writers find their voice and have their work reach the attention of readers everywhere.

The Richell Prize was established in memory of Hachette Australia's CEO, Matt Richell, who died suddenly in 2014.

 **EMERGING WRITERS' FESTIVAL** **theguardian**

The Prize has also been made possible through the support of Simpsons Solicitors and Joy.

For more information about how to enter The Richell Prize, please head to

hachette.com.au

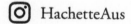
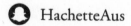